PERT Secrets

Study Guide

Your Key to Exam Success

PERT Test Review for the
Postsecondary Education Readiness Test

6/15

Dear Future Exam Success Story:

Congratulations on your purchase of our study guide. Our goal in writing our study guide was to cover the content on the test, as well as provide insight into typical test taking mistakes and how to overcome them.

Standardized tests are a key component of being successful, which only increases the importance of doing well in the high-pressure high-stakes environment of test day. How well you do on this test will have a significant impact on your future- and we have the research and practical advice to help you execute on test day.

The product you're reading now is designed to exploit weaknesses in the test itself, and help you avoid the most common errors test takers frequently make.

How to use this study guide

We don't want to waste your time. Our study guide is fast-paced and fluff-free. We suggest going through it a number of times, as repetition is an important part of learning new information and concepts.

First, read through the study guide completely to get a feel for the content and organization. Read the general success strategies first, and then proceed to the content sections. Each tip has been carefully selected for its effectiveness.

Second, read through the study guide again, and take notes in the margins and highlight those sections where you may have a particular weakness.

Finally, bring the manual with you on test day and study it before the exam begins.

Your success is our success

We would be delighted to hear about your success. Send us an email and tell us your story. Thanks for your business and we wish you continued success-

Sincerely,

Mometrix Test Preparation Team

Need more help? Check out our flashcards at: http://MometrixFlashcards.com/PERT

TABLE OF CONTENTS

Top 20 Test Taking Tips

1. Carefully follow all the test registration procedures
2. Know the test directions, duration, topics, question types, how many questions
3. Setup a flexible study schedule at least 3-4 weeks before test day
4. Study during the time of day you are most alert, relaxed, and stress free
5. Maximize your learning style; visual learner use visual study aids, auditory learner use auditory study aids
6. Focus on your weakest knowledge base
7. Find a study partner to review with and help clarify questions
8. Practice, practice, practice
9. Get a good night's sleep; don't try to cram the night before the test
10. Eat a well balanced meal
11. Know the exact physical location of the testing site; drive the route to the site prior to test day
12. Bring a set of ear plugs; the testing center could be noisy
13. Wear comfortable, loose fitting, layered clothing to the testing center; prepare for it to be either cold or hot during the test
14. Bring at least 2 current forms of ID to the testing center
15. Arrive to the test early; be prepared to wait and be patient
16. Eliminate the obviously wrong answer choices, then guess the first remaining choice
17. Pace yourself; don't rush, but keep working and move on if you get stuck
18. Maintain a positive attitude even if the test is going poorly
19. Keep your first answer unless you are positive it is wrong
20. Check your work, don't make a careless mistake

Mathematics

Numbers and Their Classifications

Numbers are the basic building blocks of mathematics. Specific features of numbers are identified by the following terms:

Integers – The set of whole positive and negative numbers, including zero. Integers do not include fractions ($\frac{1}{3}$), decimals (0.56), or mixed numbers ($7\frac{3}{4}$).

Prime number – A whole number greater than 1 that has only two factors, itself and 1; that is, a number that can be divided evenly only by 1 and itself.

Composite number – A whole number greater than 1 that has more than two different factors; in other words, any whole number that is not a prime number. For example: The composite number 8 has the factors of 1, 2, 4, and 8.

Even number – Any integer that can be divided by 2 without leaving a remainder. For example: 2, 4, 6, 8, and so on.

Odd number – Any integer that cannot be divided evenly by 2. For example: 3, 5, 7, 9, and so on.

Decimal number – a number that uses a decimal point to show the part of the number that is less than one. Example: 1.234.

Decimal point – a symbol used to separate the ones place from the tenths place in decimals or dollars from cents in currency.

Decimal place – the position of a number to the right of the decimal point. In the decimal 0.123, the 1 is in the first place to the right of the decimal point, indicating tenths; the 2 is in the second place, indicating hundredths; and the 3 is in the third place, indicating thousandths.

The decimal, or base 10, system is a number system that uses ten different digits (0, 1, 2, 3, 4, 5, 6, 7, 8, 9). An example of a number system that uses something other than ten digits is the binary, or base 2, number system, used by computers, which uses only the numbers 0 and 1. It is thought that the decimal system originated because people had only their 10 fingers for counting.

Rational, irrational, and real numbers can be described as follows:

Rational numbers include all integers, decimals, and fractions. Any terminating or repeating decimal number is a rational number.

Irrational numbers cannot be written as fractions or decimals because the number of decimal places is infinite and there is no recurring pattern of digits within the number. For example, pi (π) begins with 3.141592 and continues without terminating or repeating, so pi is an irrational number.

Real numbers are the set of all rational and irrational numbers.

> ➤ **Review Video: <u>Numbers and Their Classification</u>**
> *Visit **mometrix.com/academy** and enter **Code: 461071***

Operations

There are four basic mathematical operations:

Addition increases the value of one quantity by the value of another quantity. Example: $2 + 4 = 6; 8 + 9 = 17$. The result is called the sum. With addition, the order does not matter. $4 + 2 = 2 + 4$.

Subtraction is the opposite operation to addition; it decreases the value of one quantity by the value of another quantity. Example: $6 - 4 = 2; 17 - 8 = 9$. The result is called the difference. Note that with subtraction, the order does matter. $6 - 4 \neq 4 - 6$.

Multiplication can be thought of as repeated addition. One number tells how many times to add the other number to itself. Example: 3×2 (three times two) $= 2 + 2 + 2 = 6$. With multiplication, the order does not matter. $2 \times 3 = 3 \times 2$ or $3 + 3 = 2 + 2 + 2$.

Division is the opposite operation to multiplication; one number tells us how many parts to divide the other number into. Example: $20 \div 4 = 5$; if 20 is split into 4 equal parts, each part is 5. With division, the order of the numbers does matter. $20 \div 4 \neq 4 \div 20$.

An exponent is a superscript number placed next to another number at the top right. It indicates how many times the base number is to be multiplied by itself. Exponents provide a shorthand way to write what would be a longer mathematical expression.

Example: $a^2 = a \times a$; $2^4 = 2 \times 2 \times 2 \times 2$. A number with an exponent of 2 is said to be "squared," while a number with an exponent of 3 is said to be "cubed." The value of a number raised to an exponent is called its power. So, 8^4 is read as "8 to the 4th power," or "8 raised to the power of 4." A negative exponent is the same as the reciprocal of a positive exponent. Example: $a^{-2} = \frac{1}{a^2}$.

Parentheses are used to designate which operations should be done first when there are multiple operations. Example: 4 – (2 + 1) = 1; the parentheses tell us that we must add 2 and 1, and then subtract the sum from 4, rather than subtracting 2 from 4 and then adding 1 (this would give us an answer of 3).

Order of Operations is a set of rules that dictates the order in which we must perform each operation in an expression so that we will evaluate at accurately. If we have an expression that includes multiple different operations, Order of Operations tells us which operations to do first. The most common mnemonic for Order of Operations is PEMDAS, or "Please Excuse My Dear Aunt Sally." PEMDAS stands for Parentheses, Exponents, Multiplication, Division, Addition, Subtraction. It is important to understand that multiplication and division have equal precedence, as do addition and subtraction, so those pairs of operations are simply worked from left to right in order.

> **Review Video: Order of Operations**
> *Visit **mometrix.com/academy** and enter **Code: 259675***

Example: Evaluate the expression $5 + 20 \div 4 \times (2 + 3)^2 - 6$ using the correct order of operations.

P: Perform the operations inside the parentheses, (2 + 3) = 5.

E: Simplify the exponents, $(5)^2 = 25$.

The equation now looks like this: $5 + 20 \div 4 \times 25 - 6$.

MD: Perform multiplication and division from left to right, $20 \div 4 = 5$; then $5 \times 25 = 125$.

The equation now looks like this: $5 + 125 - 6$.

AS: Perform addition and subtraction from left to right, $5 + 125 = 130$; then $130 - 6 = 124$.

The laws of exponents are as follows:

1) Any number to the power of 1 is equal to itself: $a^1 = a$.

2) The number 1 raised to any power is equal to 1: $1^n = 1$.

3) Any number raised to the power of 0 is equal to 1: $a^0 = 1$.

4) Add exponents to multiply powers of the same base number: $a^n \times a^m = a^{n+m}$.

5) Subtract exponents to divide powers of the same number; that is $a^n \div a^m = a^{n-m}$.

6) Multiply exponents to raise a power to a power: $(a^n)^m = a^{n \times m}$.

7) If multiplied or divided numbers inside parentheses are collectively raised to a power, this is the same as each individual term being raised to that power: $(a \times b)^n = a^n \times b^n$; $(a \div b)^n = a^n \div b^n$.

Note: Exponents do not have to be integers. Fractional or decimal exponents follow all the rules above as well. Example: $5^{\frac{1}{4}} \times 5^{\frac{3}{4}} = 5^{\frac{1}{4}+\frac{3}{4}} = 5^1 = 5$.

A root, such as a square root, is another way of writing a fractional exponent. Instead of using a superscript, roots use the radical symbol ($\sqrt{}$) to indicate the operation. A radical will have a number underneath the bar, and may sometimes have a number in the upper left: $\sqrt[n]{a}$, read as "the nth root of a." The relationship between radical notation and exponent notation can be described by this equation: $\sqrt[n]{a} = a^{\frac{1}{n}}$. The two special cases of $n = 2$ and $n = 3$ are called square roots and cube roots. If there is no number to the upper left, it is understood to be a square root ($n = 2$). Nearly all of the roots you encounter will be square roots. A square root is the same as a number raised to the one-half power. When we say that a is the square root of b ($a = \sqrt{b}$), we mean that a multiplied by itself equals b: ($a \times a = b$).

A perfect square is a number that has an integer for its square root. There are 10 perfect squares from 1 to 100: 1, 4, 9, 16, 25, 36, 49, 64, 81, 100 (the squares of integers 1 through 10).

Scientific notation is a way of writing large numbers in a shorter form. The form $a \times 10^n$ is used in scientific notation, where a is greater than or equal to 1, but less than 10, and n is the number of places the decimal must move to get from the original number to a. Example:

The number 230,400,000 is cumbersome to write. To write the value in scientific notation, place a decimal point between the first and second numbers, and include all digits through the last non-zero digit ($a = 2.304$). To find the appropriate power of 10, count the number of places the decimal point had to move ($n = 8$). The number is positive if the decimal moved to the left, and negative if it moved to the right. We can then write 230,400,000 as 2.304×10^8. If we look instead at the number 0.00002304, we have the same value for a, but this time the decimal moved 5 places to the right ($n = -5$). Thus, 0.00002304 can be written as 2.304×10^{-5}. Using this notation makes it simple to compare very large or very small numbers. By comparing exponents, it is easy to see that 3.28×10^4 is smaller than 1.51×10^5, because 4 is less than 5.

Positive & Negative Numbers

A precursor to working with negative numbers is understanding what absolute values are. A number's *Absolute Value* is simply the distance away from zero a number is on the number line. The absolute value of a number is always positive and is written $|x|$.

When adding signed numbers, if the signs are the same simply add the absolute values of the addends and apply the original sign to the sum. For example, $(+4) + (+8) = +12$ and $(-4) + (-8) = -12$. When the original signs are different, take the absolute values of the addends and subtract the smaller value from the larger value, then apply the original sign of the larger value to the difference. For instance, $(+4) + (-8) = -4$ and $(-4) + (+8) = +4$.

For subtracting signed numbers, change the sign of the number after the minus symbol and then follow the same rules used for addition. For example, $(+4) - (+8) = (+4) + (-8) = -4$.

If the signs are the same the product is positive when multiplying signed numbers. For example, $(+4) \times (+8) = +32$ and $(-4) \times (-8) = +32$. If the signs are opposite, the product is negative. For example, $(+4) \times (-8) = -32$ and $(-4) \times (+8) = -32$. When more than two factors are multiplied together, the sign of the product is determined by how many negative factors are present. If there are an odd number of negative factors then the product is negative, whereas an even number of negative factors indicates a positive product. For instance, $(+4) \times (-8) \times (-2) = +64$ and $(-4) \times (-8) \times (-2) = -64$.

The rules for dividing signed numbers are similar to multiplying signed numbers. If the dividend and divisor have the same sign, the quotient is positive. If the dividend and divisor have opposite signs, the quotient is negative. For example, $(-4) \div (+8) = -0.5$.

Factors and Multiples

Factors are numbers that are multiplied together to obtain a product. For example, in the equation $2 \times 3 = 6$, the numbers 2 and 3 are factors. A prime number has only two factors (1 and itself), but other numbers can have many factors.

A common factor is a number that divides exactly into two or more other numbers. For example, the factors of 12 are 1, 2, 3, 4, 6, and 12, while the factors of 15 are 1, 3, 5, and 15. The common factors of 12 and 15 are 1 and 3.

A prime factor is also a prime number. Therefore, the prime factors of 12 are 1, 2, and 3. For 15, the prime factors are 1, 3, and 5.

> ➢ **Review Video: Factors**
> *Visit **mometrix.com/academy** and enter **Code: 920086***

The greatest common factor (GCF) is the largest number that is a factor of two or more numbers. For example, the factors of 15 are 1, 3, 5, and 15; the factors of 35 are 1, 5, 7, and 35. Therefore, the greatest common factor of 15 and 35 is 5.

The least common multiple (LCM) is the smallest number that is a multiple of two or more numbers. For example, the multiples of 3 include 3, 6, 9, 12, 15, etc.; the multiples of 5 include 5, 10, 15, 20, etc. Therefore, the least common multiple of 3 and 5 is 15.

> ➢ **Review Video: Multiples**
> *Visit **mometrix.com/academy** and enter **Code: 626738***

Fractions, Percentages, and Related Concepts

A fraction is a number that is expressed as one integer written above another integer, with a dividing line between them $\left(\frac{x}{y}\right)$. It represents the quotient of the two numbers "x divided by y." It can also be thought of as x out of y equal parts.

The top number of a fraction is called the numerator, and it represents the number of parts under consideration. The 1 in $\frac{1}{4}$ means that 1 part out of the whole is being considered in the calculation. The bottom number of a fraction is called the denominator, and it represents the total number of equal parts. The 4 in $\frac{1}{4}$ means that the whole consists of 4 equal parts. A fraction cannot have a denominator of zero; this is referred to as "undefined."

Fractions can be manipulated, without changing the value of the fraction, by multiplying or dividing (but not adding or subtracting) both the numerator and denominator by the same number. If you divide both numbers by a common factor, you are reducing or simplifying the fraction. Two fractions that have the same value, but are expressed differently are known as equivalent fractions. For example, $\frac{2}{10}, \frac{3}{15}, \frac{4}{20}$, and $\frac{5}{25}$ are all equivalent fractions. They can also all be reduced or simplified to $\frac{1}{5}$.

When two fractions are manipulated so that they have the same denominator, this is known as finding a common denominator. The number chosen to be that common denominator should be the least common multiple of the two original denominators. Example: $\frac{3}{4}$ and $\frac{5}{6}$; the least common multiple of 4 and 6 is 12. Manipulating to achieve the common denominator: $\frac{3}{4} = \frac{9}{12}; \frac{5}{6} = \frac{10}{12}$.

If two fractions have a common denominator, they can be added or subtracted simply by adding or subtracting the two numerators and retaining the same denominator. Example: $\frac{1}{2} + \frac{1}{4} = \frac{2}{4} + \frac{1}{4} = \frac{3}{4}$. If the two fractions do not already have the same denominator, one or both of them must be manipulated to achieve a common denominator before they can be added or subtracted.

Two fractions can be multiplied by multiplying the two numerators to find the new numerator and the two denominators to find the new denominator. Example: $\frac{1}{3} \times \frac{2}{3} = \frac{1 \times 2}{3 \times 3} = \frac{2}{9}$.

Two fractions can be divided flipping the numerator and denominator of the second fraction and then proceeding as though it were a multiplication. Example: $\frac{2}{3} \div \frac{3}{4} = \frac{2}{3} \times \frac{4}{3} = \frac{8}{9}$.

A fraction whose denominator is greater than its numerator is known as a proper fraction, while a fraction whose numerator is greater than its denominator is known as an improper fraction. Proper fractions have values less than one and improper fractions have values greater than one.

A mixed number is a number that contains both an integer and a fraction. Any improper fraction can be rewritten as a mixed number. Example: $\frac{8}{3} = \frac{6}{3} + \frac{2}{3} = 2 + \frac{2}{3} = 2\frac{2}{3}$. Similarly, any mixed number can be rewritten as an improper fraction. Example: $1\frac{3}{5} = 1 + \frac{3}{5} = \frac{5}{5} + \frac{3}{5} = \frac{8}{5}$.

> **Review Video: <u>Fractions</u>**
> Visit **mometrix.com/academy** and enter **Code: 262335**

Percentages can be thought of as fractions that are based on a whole of 100; that is, one whole is equal to 100%. The word percent means "per hundred." Fractions can be expressed as percents by finding equivalent fractions with a denomination of 100. Example: $\frac{7}{10} = \frac{70}{100} = 70\%$; $\frac{1}{4} = \frac{25}{100} = 25\%$.

To express a percentage as a fraction, divide the percentage number by 100 and reduce the fraction to its simplest possible terms. Example: $60\% = \frac{60}{100} = \frac{3}{5}$; $96\% = \frac{96}{100} = \frac{24}{25}$.

Converting decimals to percentages and percentages to decimals is as simple as moving the decimal point. To convert from a decimal to a percent, move the decimal point two places to the right. To convert from a percent to a decimal, move it two places to the left. Example: 0.23 = 23%; 5.34 = 534%; 0.007 = 0.7%; 700% = 7.00; 86% = 0.86; 0.15% = 0.0015. It may be helpful to remember that the percentage number will always be larger than the equivalent decimal number.

A percentage problem can be presented three main ways: (1) Find what percentage of some number another number is. Example: What percentage of 40 is 8? (2) Find what number is some percentage of a given number. Example: What number is 20% of 40? (3) Find what number another number is a given percentage of. Example: What number is 8 20% of? The three components in all of these cases are the same: a whole (W), a part (P), and a percentage (%). These are related by the equation: $P = W \times \%$. This is the form of the equation you would use to solve problems of type (2). To solve types (1) and (3), you would use these two forms: $\% = \frac{P}{W}$ and $W = \frac{P}{\%}$.

The thing that frequently makes percentage problems difficult is that they are most often also word problems, so a large part of solving them is figuring out which quantities are what. Example: In a school cafeteria, 7 students choose pizza, 9 choose hamburgers, and 4 choose tacos. Find the percentage that chooses tacos. To find the whole, you must first add all of the parts: 7 + 9 + 4 = 20. The percentage can then be found by dividing the part by the whole ($\% = \frac{P}{W}$): $\frac{4}{20} = \frac{20}{100} = 20\%$.

➢ **Review Video: Percentages**
*Visit **mometrix.com/academy** and enter **Code: 141911***

A ratio is a comparison of two quantities in a particular order. Example: If there are 14 computers in a lab, and the class has 20 students, there is a student to computer ratio of 20 to 14, commonly written as 20:14. Ratios are normally reduced to their smallest whole number representation, so 20:14 would be reduced to 10:7 by dividing both sides by 2.

A proportion is a relationship between two quantities that dictates how one changes when the other changes. A direct proportion describes a relationship in which a quantity increases by a set amount for every increase in the other quantity, or decreases by that same amount for every decrease in the other quantity. Example: Assuming a constant driving speed, the time required for a car trip increases as the distance of the trip increases. The distance to be traveled and the time required to travel are directly proportional.

Inverse proportion is a relationship in which an increase in one quantity is accompanied by a decrease in the other, or vice versa. Example: the time required for a car trip decreases as the speed increases, and increases as the speed decreases, so the time required is inversely proportional to the speed of the car.

Equations and Graphing

When algebraic functions and equations are shown graphically, they are usually shown on a *Cartesian Coordinate Plane*. The Cartesian coordinate plane consists of two number lines placed perpendicular to each other, and intersecting at the zero point, also known as the origin. The horizontal number line is known as the x-axis, with positive values to the right of the origin, and negative values to the left of the origin. The vertical number line is known as the y-axis, with positive values above the origin, and negative values below the origin. Any point on the plane can be identified by an ordered pair in the form (x,y), called coordinates. The x-value of the coordinate is called the abscissa, and the y-value of the coordinate is called the ordinate. The two number lines divide the plane into four quadrants: I, II, III, and IV.

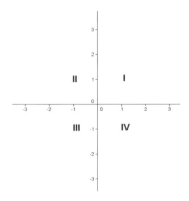

Before learning the different forms equations can be written in, it is important to understand some terminology. A ratio of the change in the vertical distance to the change in horizontal distance is called the *Slope*. On a graph with two points, (x_1, y_1) and (x_2, y_2), the slope is represented by the formula $= \frac{y_2 - y_1}{x_2 - x_1}$; $x_1 \neq x_2$. If the value of the slope is positive, the line slopes upward from left to right. If the value of the slope is negative, the line slopes downward from left to right. If the y-coordinates are the same for both points, the slope is 0 and the line is a *Horizontal Line*. If the x-coordinates are the same for both points, there is no slope and the line is a *Vertical Line*. Two or more lines that have equal slopes are *Parallel*

Lines. Perpendicular Lines have slopes that are negative reciprocals of each other, such as $\frac{a}{b}$ and $\frac{-b}{a}$.

Equations are made up of monomials and polynomials. A *Monomial* is a single variable or product of constants and variables, such as x, $2x$, or $\frac{2}{x}$. There will never be addition or subtraction symbols in a monomial. Like monomials have like variables, but they may have different coefficients. *Polynomials* are algebraic expressions which use addition and subtraction to combine two or more monomials. Two terms make a binomial; three terms make a trinomial; etc.. The *Degree of a Monomial* is the sum of the exponents of the variables. The *Degree of a Polynomial* is the highest degree of any individual term.

As mentioned previously, equations can be written many ways. Below is a list of the many forms equations can take.

- *Standard Form*: $Ax + By = C$; the slope is $\frac{-A}{B}$ and the y-intercept is $\frac{C}{B}$
- *Slope Intercept Form*: $y = mx + b$, where m is the slope and b is the y-intercept
- *Point-Slope Form*: $y - y_1 = m(x - x_1)$, where m is the slope and (x_1, y_1) is a point on the line
- *Two-Point Form*: $\frac{y - y_1}{x - x_1} = \frac{y_2 - y_1}{x_2 - x_1}$, where (x_1, y_1) and (x_2, y_2) are two points on the given line
- *Intercept Form*: $\frac{x}{x_1} + \frac{y}{y_1} = 1$, where $(x_1, 0)$ is the point at which a line intersects the x-axis, and $(0, y_1)$ is the point at which the same line intersects the y-axis

Equations can also be written as $ax + b = 0$, where $a \neq 0$. These are referred to as *One Variable Linear Equations*. A solution to such an equation is called a *Root*. In the case where we have the equation $5x + 10 = 0$, if we solve for x we get a solution of $x = -2$. In other words, the root of the equation is -2. This is found by first subtracting 10 from both sides, which gives $5x = -10$. Next, simply divide both sides by the coefficient of the variable, in this case 5, to get $x = -2$. This can be checked by plugging -2 back into the original equation $(5)(-2) + 10 = -10 + 10 = 0$.

The *Solution Set* is the set of all solutions of an equation. In our example, the solution set would simply be -2. If there were more solutions (there usually are in multivariable equations) then they would also be included in the solution set. When an equation has no true solutions, this is referred to as an *Empty Set*. Equations with identical solution sets are *Equivalent Equations*. An *Identity* is a term whose value or determinant is equal to 1.

Other Important Concepts

Commonly in algebra and other upper-level fields of math you find yourself working with mathematical expressions that do not equal each other. The statement comparing such expressions with symbols such as < (less than) or > (greater than) is called an *Inequality*. An example of an inequality is $7x > 5$. To solve for x, simply divide both sides by 7 and the solution is shown to be $x > \frac{5}{7}$. Graphs of the solution set of inequalities are represented on a number line. Open circles are used to show that an expression approaches a number but is never quite equal to that number.

Conditional Inequalities are those with certain values for the variable that will make the condition true and other values for the variable where the condition will be false. *Absolute Inequalities* can have any real number as the value for the variable to make the condition true, while there is no real number value for the variable that will make the condition false. Solving inequalities is done by following the same rules as for solving equations with the exception that when multiplying or dividing by a negative number the direction of the inequality sign must be flipped or reversed. *Double Inequalities* are situations where two inequality statements apply to the same variable expression. An example of this is $-c < ax + b < c$.

A *Weighted Mean*, or weighted average, is a mean that uses "weighted" values. The formula is weighted mean $= \frac{w_1 x_1 + w_2 x_2 + w_3 x_3 \dots + w_n x_n}{w_1 + w_2 + w_3 + \dots + w_n}$. Weighted values, such as $w_1, w_2, w_3, \dots w_n$ are assigned to each member of the set $x_1, x_2, x_3, \dots x_n$. If calculating weighted mean, make sure a weight value for each member of the set is used.

Calculations Using Points

Sometimes you need to perform calculations using only points on a graph as input data. Using points, you can determine what the midpoint and distance are. If you know the equation for a line you can calculate the distance between the line and the point.

To find the *Midpoint* of two points (x_1, y_1) and (x_2, y_2), average the x-coordinates to get the x-coordinate of the midpoint, and average the y-coordinates to get the y-coordinate of the midpoint. The formula is midpoint $= \left(\frac{x_1+x_2}{2}, \frac{y_1+y_2}{2}\right)$.

The *Distance* between two points is the same as the length of the hypotenuse of a right triangle with the two given points as endpoints, and the two sides of the right triangle parallel to the x-axis and y-axis, respectively. The length of the segment parallel to the x-axis is the difference between the x-coordinates of the two points. The length of the segment parallel to the y-axis is the difference between the y-coordinates of the two points. Use the Pythagorean Theorem $a^2 + b^2 = c^2$ or $c = \sqrt{a^2 + b^2}$ to find the distance. The formula is: distance $= \sqrt{(x_2 - x_1)^2 + (y_2 - y_1)^2}$.

When a line is in the format $Ax + By + C = 0$, where A, B, and C are coefficients, you can use a point (x_1, y_1) not on the line and apply the formula $d = \frac{|Ax_1 + By_1 + C|}{\sqrt{A^2 + B^2}}$ to find the distance between the line and the point (x_1, y_1).

Systems of Equations

Systems of Equations are a set of simultaneous equations that all use the same variables. A solution to a system of equations must be true for each equation in the system. *Consistent Systems* are those with at least one solution. *Inconsistent Systems* are systems of equations that have no solution.

To solve a system of linear equations by *substitution*, start with the easier equation and solve for one of the variables. Express this variable in terms of the other variable. Substitute this expression in the other equation, and solve for the other variable. The solution should be expressed in the form (x, y). Substitute the values into both of the original equations to check your answer. Consider the following problem.

Solve the system using substitution:

$x + 6y = 15$

$3x - 12y = 18$

Solve the first equation for x:

$x = 15 - 6y$

Substitute this value in place of x in the second equation, and solve for y:

$3(15 - 6y) - 12y = 18$

$45 - 18y - 12y = 18$

$30y = 27$

$y = \dfrac{27}{30} = \dfrac{9}{10} = 0.9$

Plug this value for y back into the first equation to solve for x:

$x = 15 - 6(0.9) = 15 - 5.4 = 9.6$

Check both equations if you have time:

$9.6 + 6(0.9) = 9.6 + 5.4 = 15$

$3(9.6) - 12(0.9) = 28.8 - 10.8 = 18$

Therefore, the solution is $(9.6, 0.9)$.

To solve a system of equations using *elimination*, begin by rewriting both equations in standard form $Ax + By = C$. Check to see if the coefficients of one pair of like variables add to zero. If not, multiply one or both of the equations by a non-zero number to make one set of like variables add to zero. Add the two equations to solve for one of the variables. Substitute this value into one of the original equations to solve for the other variable. Check your work by substituting into the other equation. Next we will solve the same problem as above, but using the addition method.

Solve the system using elimination:

$x + 6y = 15$

$3x - 12y = 18$

If we multiply the first equation by 2, we can eliminate the y terms:

$2x + 12y = 30$

$3x - 12y = 18$

Add the equations together and solve for x:

$5x = 48$

$x = \dfrac{48}{5} = 9.6$

Plug the value for x back into either of the original equations and solve for y:

$9.6 + 6y = 15$

$y = \dfrac{15 - 9.6}{6} = 0.9$

Check both equations if you have time:

$9.6 + 6(0.9) = 9.6 + 5.4 = 15$

$3(9.6) - 12(0.9) = 28.8 - 10.8 = 18$

Therefore, the solution is (9.6, 0.9).

> ➤ **Review Video: <u>System of Equations</u>**
> *Visit **mometrix.com/academy** and enter **Code: 658153***

Polynomial Algebra

To multiply two binomials, follow the *FOIL* method. FOIL stands for:

1. First: Multiply the first term of each binomial
2. Outer: Multiply the outer terms of each binomial
3. Inner: Multiply the inner terms of each binomial
4. Last: Multiply the last term of each binomial

Using FOIL $(Ax + By)(Cx + Dy) = ACx^2 + ADxy + BCxy + BDy^2$.

To divide polynomials, begin by arranging the terms of each polynomial in order of one variable. You may arrange in ascending or descending order, but be consistent with both polynomials. To get the first term of the quotient, divide the first term of the dividend by the first term of the divisor. Multiply the first term of the quotient by the entire divisor and subtract that product from the dividend. Repeat for the second and successive terms until you either get a remainder of zero or a remainder whose degree is less than the degree of the divisor. If the quotient has a remainder, write the answer as a mixed expression in the form: quotient $+ \frac{\text{remainder}}{\text{divisor}}$.

Rational Expressions are fractions with polynomials in both the numerator and the denominator; the value of the polynomial in the denominator cannot be equal to zero. To add or subtract rational expressions, first find the common denominator, then rewrite each fraction as an equivalent fraction with the common denominator. Finally, add or subtract the numerators to get the numerator of the answer, and keep the common denominator as the denominator of the answer. When multiplying rational expressions factor each polynomial and cancel like factors (a factor which appears in both the numerator and the denominator). Then, multiply all remaining factors in the numerator to get the numerator of the product, and multiply the remaining factors in the denominator to get the denominator of the product. Remember – cancel entire factors, not individual terms. To divide rational expressions, take the reciprocal of the divisor (the rational expression you are dividing by) and multiply by the dividend.

Below are patterns of some special products to remember: *perfect trinomial squares*, the *difference between two squares*, the *sum and difference of two cubes*, and *perfect cubes*.

- Perfect Trinomial Squares: $x^2 + 2xy + y^2 = (x + y)^2$ or $x^2 - 2xy + y^2 = (x - y)^2$
- Difference Between Two Squares: $x^2 - y^2 = (x + y)(x - y)$
- Sum of Two Cubes: $x^3 + y^3 = (x + y)(x^2 - xy + y^2)$
  Note: the second factor is NOT the same as a perfect trinomial square, so do not try to factor it further.

- Difference between Two Cubes: $x^3 - y^3 = (x - y)(x^2 + xy + y^2)$

  Again, the second factor is NOT the same as a perfect trinomial square.
- Perfect Cubes: $x^3 + 3x^2y + 3xy^2 + y^3 = (x + y)^3$ and $x^3 - 3x^2y + 3xy^2 - y^3 = (x - y)^3$

In order to *factor* a polynomial, first check for a common monomial factor. When the greatest common monomial factor has been factored out, look for patterns of special products: differences of two squares, the sum or difference of two cubes for binomial factors, or perfect trinomial squares for trinomial factors. If the factor is a trinomial but not a perfect trinomial square, look for a factorable form, such as $x^2 + (a + b)x + ab = (x + a)(x + b)$ or $(ac)x^2 + (ad + bc)x + bd = (ax + b)(cx + d)$. For factors with four terms, look for groups to factor. Once you have found the factors, write the original polynomial as the product of all the factors. Make sure all of the polynomial factors are prime. Monomial factors may be prime or composite. Check your work by multiplying the factors to make sure you get the original polynomial.

Solving Quadratic Equations

The *Quadratic Formula* is used to solve quadratic equations when other methods are more difficult. To use the quadratic formula to solve a quadratic equation, begin by rewriting the equation in standard form $ax^2 + bx + c = 0$, where a, b, and c are coefficients. Once you have identified the values of the coefficients, substitute those values into the quadratic formula $= \frac{-b \pm \sqrt{b^2 - 4ac}}{2a}$. Evaluate the equation and simplify the expression. Again, check each root by substituting into the original equation. In the quadratic formula, the portion of the formula under the radical ($b^2 - 4ac$) is called the *Discriminant*. If the discriminant is zero, there is only one root: zero. If the discriminant is positive, there are two different real roots. If the discriminant is negative, there are no real roots.

> ➤ **Review Video:** <u>**Using the Quadratic Formula**</u>
> *Visit **mometrix.com/academy** and enter **Code:** 163102*

To solve a quadratic equation by *Factoring*, begin by rewriting the equation in standard form, if necessary. Factor the side with the variable then set each of the factors equal to zero and solve the resulting linear equations. Check your answers by substituting the roots you found into the original equation. If, when writing the equation in standard form, you have an equation in the form $x^2 + c = 0$ or $x^2 - c = 0$, set $x^2 = -c$ or $x^2 = c$ and take the square root of c. If $c = 0$, the only real root is zero. If c is positive, there are two real roots—the positive and negative square root values. If c is negative, there are no real roots because you cannot take the square root of a negative number.

To solve a quadratic equation by *Completing the Square*, rewrite the equation so that all terms containing the variable are on the left side of the equal sign, and all the constants are on the right side of the equal sign. Make sure the coefficient of the squared term is 1. If there is a coefficient with the squared term, divide each term on both sides of the equal side by that number. Next, work with the coefficient of the single-variable term. Square half of this coefficient, and add that value to both sides. Now you can factor the left side (the side containing the variable) as the square of a binomial. $x^2 + 2ax + a^2 = C \Rightarrow (x + a)^2 = C$, where x is the variable, and a and C are constants. Take the square root of both sides and solve for the variable. Substitute the value of the variable in the original problem to check your work.

Reading

Important Skills

One of the most important skills in reading comprehension is the identification of **topics** and **main ideas.** There is a subtle difference between these two features. The topic is the subject of a text, or what the text is about. The main idea, on the other hand, is the most important point being made by the author. The topic is usually expressed in a few words at the most, while the main idea often needs a full sentence to be completely defined. As an example, a short passage might have the topic of penguins and the main idea *Penguins are different from other birds in many ways.* In most nonfiction writing, the topic and the main idea will be stated directly, often in a sentence at the very beginning or end of the text. When being tested on an understanding of the author's topic, the reader can quickly *skim* the passage for the general idea, stopping to read only the first sentence of each paragraph. A paragraph's first sentence is often (but not always) the main topic sentence, and it gives you a summary of the content of the paragraph. However, there are cases in which the reader must figure out an unstated topic or main idea. In these instances, the student must read every sentence of the text, and try to come up with an overarching idea that is supported by each of those sentences.

> ➤ **Review Video: <u>Topics and Main Ideas</u>**
> *Visit **mometrix.com/academy** and enter **Code: 407801***

While the main idea is the overall premise of a story, **supporting details** provide evidence and backing for the main point. In order to show that a main idea is correct, or valid, the author needs to add details that prove their point. All texts contain details, but they are only classified as supporting details when they serve to reinforce some larger point. Supporting details are most commonly found in informative and persuasive texts. In some cases, they will be clearly indicated with words like *for example* or *for instance*, or they will be enumerated with words like *first*, *second*, and *last*. However, they may not be indicated with special words. As a reader, it is important to consider whether the author's supporting details really back up his or her main point. Supporting details can be factual and correct but still not relevant to the author's point. Conversely, supporting details can seem pertinent but be ineffective because they are based on opinion or assertions that cannot be proven.

An example of a main idea is: "Giraffes live in the Serengeti of Africa." A supporting detail about giraffes could be: "A giraffe uses its long neck to reach twigs and leaves on trees." The main idea gives the general idea that the text is about giraffes. The supporting detail gives a specific fact about how the giraffes eat.

> **Review Video: <u>Supporting Details</u>**
> *Visit **mometrix.com/academy** and enter **Code: 396297***

As opposed to a main idea, themes are seldom expressed directly in a text, so they can be difficult to identify. A **theme** is an issue, an idea, or a question raised by the text. For instance, a theme of William Shakespeare's *Hamlet* is indecision, as the title character explores his own psyche and the results of his failure to make bold choices. A great work of literature may have many themes, and the reader is justified in identifying any for which he or she can find support. One common characteristic of themes is that they raise more questions than they answer. In a good piece of fiction, the author is not always trying to convince the reader, but is instead trying to elevate the reader's perspective and encourage him to consider the themes more deeply.

When reading, one can identify themes by constantly asking what general issues the text is addressing. A good way to evaluate an author's approach to a theme is to begin reading with a question in mind (for example, how does this text approach the theme of love?) and then look for evidence in the text that addresses that question.

> **Review Video: <u>Theme</u>**
> *Visit **mometrix.com/academy** and enter **Code: 732074***

Purposes for Writing

In order to be an effective reader, one must pay attention to the author's **position** and purpose. Even those texts that seem objective and impartial, like textbooks, have some sort of position and bias. Readers need to take these positions into account when considering the author's message. When an author uses emotional language or clearly favors one side of an argument, his position is clear. However, the author's position may be evident not only in what he writes, but in what he doesn't write. For this reason, it is sometimes necessary to review some other texts on the same topic in order to develop a view of the author's position. If this is not possible, then it may be useful to acquire a little background personal information about the author. When the only source of information is the text, however, the reader should look for language and argumentation that seems to indicate a particular stance on the subject.

> ➢ **Review Video: <u>Author's Position</u>**
> *Visit **mometrix.com/academy** and enter **Code: 827954***

Identifying the **purpose** of an author is usually easier than identifying her position. In most cases, the author has no interest in hiding his or her purpose. A text that is meant to entertain, for instance, should be obviously written to please the reader. Most narratives, or stories, are written to entertain, though they may also inform or persuade. Informative texts are easy to identify as well. The most difficult purpose of a text to identify is persuasion, because the author has an interest in making this purpose hard to detect. When a person knows that the author is trying to convince him, he is automatically more wary and skeptical of the argument. For this reason persuasive texts often try to establish an entertaining tone, hoping to amuse the reader into agreement, or an informative tone, hoping to create an appearance of authority and objectivity.

> ➢ **Review Video: <u>Purpose</u>**
> *Visit **mometrix.com/academy** and enter **Code: 511819***

An author's purpose is often evident in the organization of the text. For instance, if the text has headings and subheadings, if key terms are in bold, and if the author makes his main idea clear from the beginning, then the likely purpose of the text is to inform. If the author begins by making a claim and then makes various arguments to support that claim, the purpose is probably to persuade. If the author is telling a story, or is more interested in holding the attention of the reader than in making a particular point or delivering information, then his purpose is most likely to entertain. As a reader, it is best to judge an author on how well he accomplishes his purpose. In other words, it is not entirely fair to complain that a textbook is boring: if the text is clear and easy to understand, then the author has done his job. Similarly, a storyteller should not be judged too harshly for getting some facts wrong, so long as he is able to give pleasure to the reader.

The author's purpose for writing will affect his writing style and the response of the reader. In a **persuasive essay**, the author is attempting to change the reader's mind or convince him of something he did not believe previously. There are several identifying characteristics of persuasive writing. One is opinion presented as fact. When an author attempts to persuade the reader, he often presents his or her opinions as if they were fact. A reader must be on guard for statements that sound factual but which cannot be subjected to research, observation, or experiment. Another characteristic of persuasive writing is emotional language. An author will often try to play on the reader's emotion by appealing to his sympathy or sense of morality. When an author uses colorful or evocative language with the intent of arousing the reader's passions, it is likely that he is attempting to persuade. Finally, in many cases a persuasive text will give an unfair explanation of opposing positions, if these positions are mentioned at all.

> ➢ **Review Video:** Persuasive Essay
> *Visit **mometrix.com/academy** and enter **Code: 621428***

An **informative text** is written to educate and enlighten the reader. Informative texts are almost always nonfiction, and are rarely structured as a story. The intention of an informative text is to deliver information in the most comprehensible way possible, so the structure of the text is likely to be very clear. In an informative text, the thesis statement is often in the first sentence. The author may use some colorful language, but is likely to put more emphasis on clarity and precision. Informative essays do not typically appeal to the emotions. They often contain facts and figures, and rarely include the opinion of the author. Sometimes a persuasive essay can resemble an informative essay, especially if the author maintains an even tone and presents his or her views as if they were established fact.

> ➢ **Review Video:** Informative Text
> *Visit **mometrix.com/academy** and enter **Code: 924964***

The success or failure of an author's intent to **entertain** is determined by those who read the author's work. Entertaining texts may be either fiction or nonfiction, and they may describe real or imagined people, places, and events. Entertaining texts are often narratives, or stories. A text that is written to entertain is likely to contain colorful language that engages the imagination and the emotions. Such writing often features a great deal of figurative language, which typically enlivens its subject matter with images and analogies. Though an entertaining text is not usually written to persuade or inform, it may accomplish both of these tasks.

An entertaining text may appeal to the reader's emotions and cause him or her to think differently about a particular subject. In any case, entertaining texts tend to showcase the personality of the author more so than do other types of writing.

> ➤ **Review Video:** <u>Entertainment Texts</u>
> *Visit mometrix.com/academy and enter Code:* **532184**

When an author intends to **express feelings,** she may use colorful and evocative language. An author may write emotionally for any number of reasons. Sometimes, the author will do so because she is describing a personal situation of great pain or happiness. Sometimes an author is attempting to persuade the reader, and so will use emotion to stir up the passions. It can be easy to identify this kind of expression when the writer uses phrases like *I felt* and *I sense*. However, sometimes the author will simply describe feelings without introducing them. As a reader, it is important to recognize when an author is expressing emotion, and not to become overwhelmed by sympathy or passion. A reader should maintain some detachment so that he or she can still evaluate the strength of the author's argument or the quality of the writing.

> ➤ **Review Video:** <u>Express Feelings</u>
> *Visit mometrix.com/academy and enter Code:* **759390**

In a sense, almost all writing is descriptive, insofar as it seeks to describe events, ideas, or people to the reader. Some texts, however, are primarily concerned with **description**. A descriptive text focuses on a particular subject, and attempts to depict it in a way that will be clear to the reader. Descriptive texts contain many adjectives and adverbs, words that give shades of meaning and create a more detailed mental picture for the reader. A descriptive text fails when it is unclear or vague to the reader. On the other hand, however, a descriptive text that compiles too much detail can be boring and overwhelming to the reader.

A descriptive text will certainly be informative, and it may be persuasive and entertaining as well. Descriptive writing is a challenge for the author, but when it is done well, it can be fun to read.

> **Review Video: Rhetorical Strategy of Description**
> Visit *mometrix.com/academy* and enter **Code: 639813**

Writing Devices

Authors will use different stylistic and writing devices to make their meaning more clearly understood. One of those devices is comparison and contrast. When an author describes the ways in which two things are alike, he or she is **comparing** them. When the author describes the ways in which two things are different, he or she is **contrasting** them. The "compare and contrast" essay is one of the most common forms in nonfiction. It is often signaled with certain words: a comparison may be indicated with such words as *both, same, like, too,* and *as well*; while a contrast may be indicated by words like *but, however, on the other hand, instead,* and *yet*. Of course, comparisons and contrasts may be implicit without using any such signaling language. A single sentence may both compare and contrast. Consider the sentence *Brian and Sheila love ice cream, but Brian prefers vanilla and Sheila prefers strawberry.* In one sentence, the author has described both a similarity (love of ice cream) and a difference (favorite flavor).

> **Review Video: Rhetorical Strategy of Comparing and Contrasting Analysis**
> Visit *mometrix.com/academy* and enter **Code: 587299**

One of the most common text structures is **cause and effect**. A cause is an act or event that makes something happen, and an effect is the thing that happens as a result of that cause. A cause-and-effect relationship is not always explicit, but there are some words in English that signal causality, such as *since, because,* and *as a result*. As an example, consider the sentence *Because the sky was clear, Ron did not bring an umbrella.* The cause is the clear sky, and the effect is that Ron did not bring an umbrella. However, sometimes the cause-and-effect relationship will not be clearly noted. For instance, the sentence *He was late and missed the meeting* does not contain any signaling words, but it still contains a cause (he was late) and an effect (he missed the meeting). It is possible for a single cause to have multiple effects, or for a single effect to have multiple causes. Also, an effect can in turn be the cause of another effect, in what is known as a cause-and-effect chain.

> **Review Video: Rhetorical Strategy of Cause and Effect Analysis**
> *Visit mometrix.com/academy and enter Code:* **725944**

Authors often use analogies to add meaning to the text. An **analogy** is a comparison of two things. The words in the analogy are connected by a certain, often undetermined relationship. Look at this analogy: moo is to cow as quack is to duck. This analogy compares the sound that a cow makes with the sound that a duck makes. Even if the word 'quack' was not given, one could figure out it is the correct word to complete the analogy based on the relationship between the words 'moo' and 'cow'. Some common relationships for analogies include synonyms, antonyms, part to whole, definition, and actor to action.

Another element that impacts a text is the author's point of view. The **point of view** of a text is the perspective from which it is told. The author will always have a point of view about a story before he draws up a plot line. The author will know what events they want to take place, how they want the characters to interact, and how the story will resolve. An author will also have an opinion on the topic, or series of events, which is presented in the story, based on their own prior experience and beliefs.

> **Review Video: Point of View**
> *Visit mometrix.com/academy and enter Code:* **383336**

The two main points of view that authors use are first person and third person. If the narrator of the story is also the main character, or *protagonist*, the text is written in first-person point of view. In first person, the author writes with the word *I*.

Third-person point of view is probably the most common point of view that authors use. Using third person, authors refer to each character using the words *he* or *she.* In third-

- 26 -

person omniscient, the narrator is not a character in the story and tells the story of all of the characters at the same time.

A good writer will use **transitional words** and phrases to guide the reader through the text. You are no doubt familiar with the common transitions, though you may never have considered how they operate. Some transitional phrases (*after, before, during, in the middle of*) give information about time. Some indicate that an example is about to be given (*for example, in fact, for instance*). Writers use them to compare (*also, likewise*) and contrast (*however, but, yet*). Transitional words and phrases can suggest addition (*and, also, furthermore, moreover*) and logical relationships (*if, then, therefore, as a result, since*). Finally, transitional words and phrases can demarcate the steps in a process (*first, second, last*). You should incorporate transitional words and phrases where they will orient your reader and illuminate the structure of your composition.

> ➢ **Review Video: <u>Transitional Words and Phrases</u>**
> Visit ***mometrix.com/academy*** *and enter* ***Code: 197796***

Types of Passages

A **narrative** passage is a story. Narratives can be fiction or nonfiction. However, there are a few elements that a text must have in order to be classified as a narrative. To begin with, the text must have a plot. That is, it must describe a series of events.

> ➢ **Review Video: <u>Narratives</u>**
> Visit ***mometrix.com/academy*** *and enter* ***Code: 280100***

If it is a good narrative, these events will be interesting and emotionally engaging to the reader. A narrative also has characters. These could be people, animals, or even inanimate objects, so long as they participate in the plot. A narrative passage often contains figurative language, which is meant to stimulate the imagination of the reader by making comparisons and observations.

A metaphor, which is a description of one thing in terms of another, is a common piece of figurative language. *The moon was a frosty snowball* is an example of a metaphor: it is obviously untrue in the literal sense, but it suggests a certain mood for the reader. Narratives often proceed in a clear sequence, but they do not need to do so.

An **expository** passage aims to inform and enlighten the reader. It is nonfiction and usually centers around a simple, easily defined topic. Since the goal of exposition is to teach, such a passage should be as clear as possible. It is common for an expository passage to contain helpful organizing words, like *first, next, for example*, and *therefore*. These words keep the reader oriented in the text. Although expository passages do not need to feature colorful language and artful writing, they are often more effective when they do. For a reader, the challenge of expository passages is to maintain steady attention. Expository passages are not always about subjects in which a reader will naturally be interested, and the writer is often more concerned with clarity and comprehensibility than with engaging the reader. For this reason, many expository passages are dull. Making notes is a good way to maintain focus when reading an expository passage.

> ➢ **Review Video: Expository Passages**
> *Visit **mometrix.com/academy** and enter Code:* **256515**

A **technical** passage is written to describe a complex object or process. Technical writing is common in medical and technological fields, in which complicated mathematical, scientific, and engineering ideas need to be explained simply and clearly. To ease comprehension, a technical passage usually proceeds in a very logical order. Technical passages often have clear headings and subheadings, which are used to keep the reader oriented in the text. It is also common for these passages to break sections up with numbers or letters.

Many technical passages look more like an outline than a piece of prose. The amount of jargon or difficult vocabulary will vary in a technical passage depending on the intended audience. As much as possible, technical passages try to avoid language that the reader will have to research in order to understand the message. Of course, it is not always possible to avoid jargon.

> ➢ **Review Video: A Technical Passage**
> *Visit **mometrix.com/academy** and enter Code:* **478923**

A **persuasive** passage is meant to change the reader's mind or lead her into agreement with the author. The persuasive intent may be obvious, or it may be quite difficult to discern. In some cases, a persuasive passage will be indistinguishable from an informative passage: it will make an assertion and offer supporting details. However, a persuasive passage is more likely to make claims based on opinion and to appeal to the reader's emotions. Persuasive passages may not describe alternate positions and, when they do, they often display significant bias. It may be clear that a persuasive passage is giving the author's viewpoint, or the passage may adopt a seemingly objective tone. A persuasive passage is successful if it can make a convincing argument and win the trust of the reader.

> ➢ **Review Video: <u>Persuasive Text and Bias</u>**
> *Visit **mometrix.com/academy** and enter **Code: 479856***

A persuasive essay will likely focus on one central argument, but it may make many smaller claims along the way. These are subordinate arguments with which the reader must agree if he or she is going to agree with the central argument. The central argument will only be as strong as the subordinate claims. These claims should be rooted in fact and observation, rather than subjective judgment. The best persuasive essays provide enough supporting detail to justify claims without overwhelming the reader. Remember that a fact must be susceptible to independent verification: that is, it must be something the reader could confirm. Also, statistics are only effective when they take into account possible objections. For instance, a statistic on the number of foreclosed houses would only be useful if it was taken over a defined interval and in a defined area. Most readers are wary of statistics, because they are so often misleading. If possible, a persuasive essay should always include references so that the reader can obtain more information. Of course, this means that the writer's accuracy and fairness may be judged by the inquiring reader.

> ➢ **Review Video: <u>Persuasive Essay</u>**
> *Visit **mometrix.com/academy** and enter **Code: 621428***

Opinions are formed by emotion as well as reason, and persuasive writers often appeal to the feelings of the reader. Although readers should always be skeptical of this technique, it is often used in a proper and ethical manner. For instance, there are many subjects that have an obvious emotional component, and therefore cannot be completely treated without an appeal to the emotions. Consider an article on drunk driving: it makes sense to include some specific examples that will alarm or sadden the reader. After all, drunk driving often has serious and tragic consequences. Emotional appeals are not appropriate, however, when they attempt to mislead the reader. For instance, in political advertisements it is common to emphasize the patriotism of the preferred candidate, because this will encourage the audience to link their own positive feelings about the country with their opinion of the candidate. However, these ads often imply that the other candidate is unpatriotic, which in most cases is far from the truth. Another common and improper emotional appeal is the use of loaded language, as for instance referring to an avidly religious person as a "fanatic" or a passionate environmentalist as a "tree hugger." These terms introduce an emotional component that detracts from the argument.

History and Culture

Historical context has a profound influence on literature: the events, knowledge base, and assumptions of an author's time color every aspect of his or her work. Sometimes, authors hold opinions and use language that would be considered inappropriate or immoral in a modern setting, but that was acceptable in the author's time. As a reader, one should consider how the historical context influenced a work and also how today's opinions and ideas shape the way modern readers read the works of the past. For instance, in most societies of the past, women were treated as second-class citizens. An author who wrote in 18th-century England might sound sexist to modern readers, even if that author was relatively feminist in his time. Readers should not have to excuse the faulty assumptions and prejudices of the past, but they should appreciate that a person's thoughts and words are, in part, a result of the time and culture in which they live or lived, and it is perhaps unfair to expect writers to avoid all of the errors of their times.

Even a brief study of world literature suggests that writers from vastly different cultures address similar themes. For instance, works like the *Odyssey* and *Hamlet* both tackle the individual's battle for self-control and independence. In every culture, authors address themes of personal growth and the struggle for maturity. Another universal theme is the conflict between the individual and society. In works as culturally disparate as *Native Son*, the *Aeneid*, and *1984*, authors dramatize how people struggle to maintain their personalities and dignity in large, sometimes oppressive groups. Finally, many cultures have versions of the hero's (or heroine's) journey, in which an adventurous person must overcome many obstacles in order to gain greater knowledge, power, and perspective. Some famous works that treat this theme are the *Epic of Gilgamesh*, Dante's *Divine Comedy*, and *Don Quixote*.

Authors from different genres (for instance poetry, drama, novel, short story) and cultures may address similar themes, but they often do so quite differently. For instance, poets are likely to address subject matter obliquely, through the use of images and allusions. In a play, on the other hand, the author is more likely to dramatize themes by using characters to express opposing viewpoints. This disparity is known as a dialectical approach. In a novel, the author does not need to express themes directly; rather, they can be illustrated through events and actions. In some regional literatures, like those of Greece or England, authors use more irony: their works have characters that express views and make decisions that are clearly disapproved of by the author. In Latin America, there is a great tradition of using supernatural events to illustrate themes about real life. In China and Japan, authors frequently use well-established regional forms (haiku, for instance) to organize their treatment of universal themes.

Responding to Literature

When reading good literature, the reader is moved to engage actively in the text. One part of being an active reader involves making predictions. A **prediction** is a guess about what will happen next. Readers are constantly making predictions based on what they have read and what they already know.

> ➤ **Review Video: <u>Predictions</u>**
> Visit *mometrix.com/academy* and enter *Code:* **437248**

Consider the following sentence: *Staring at the computer screen in shock, Kim blindly reached over for the brimming glass of water on the shelf to her side.* The sentence suggests that Kim is agitated and that she is not looking at the glass she is going to pick up, so a reader might predict that she is going to knock the glass over. Of course, not every prediction will be accurate: perhaps Kim will pick the glass up cleanly. Nevertheless, the author has certainly created the expectation that the water might be spilled. Predictions are always subject to revision as the reader acquires more information.

Test-taking tip: To respond to questions requiring future predictions, the student's answers should be based on evidence of past or present behavior.

Readers are often required to understand text that claims and suggests ideas without stating them directly. An **inference** is a piece of information that is implied but not written outright by the author. For instance, consider the following sentence: *Mark made more money that week than he had in the previous year*. From this sentence, the reader can infer that Mark either has not made much money in the previous year or made a great deal of money that week.

Often, a reader can use information he or she already knows to make inferences. Take as an example the sentence *When his coffee arrived, he looked around the table for the silver cup*. Many people know that cream is typically served in a silver cup, so using their own base of knowledge they can infer that the subject of this sentence takes his coffee with cream. Making inferences requires concentration, attention, and practice.

> ➢ **Review Video: Inference**
> *Visit **mometrix.com/academy** and enter **Code: 379203**

Test-taking tip: While being tested on his ability to make correct inferences, the student must look for contextual clues. An answer can be *true* but not *correct*. The contextual clues will help you find the answer that is the best answer out of the given choices. Understand the context in which a phrase is stated. When asked for the implied meaning of a statement made in the passage, the student should immediately locate the statement and read the context in which it was made. Also, look for an answer choice that has a similar phrase to the statement in question.

A reader must be able to identify a text's **sequence**, or the order in which things happen. Often, and especially when the sequence is very important to the author, it is indicated with signal words like *first, then, next,* and *last.* However, sometimes a sequence is merely implied and must be noted by the reader. Consider the sentence *He walked in the front door and switched on the hall lamp.* Clearly, the man did not turn the lamp on before he walked in the door, so the implied sequence is that he first walked in the door and then turned on the lamp. Texts do not always proceed in an orderly sequence from first to last: sometimes, they begin at the end and then start over at the beginning. As a reader, it can be useful to make brief notes to clarify the sequence.

> ➤ **Review Video: <u>Sequence</u>**
> *Visit **mometrix.com/academy** and enter **Code: 489027***

In addition to inferring and predicting things about the text, the reader must often **draw conclusions** about the information he has read. When asked for a *conclusion* that may be drawn, look for critical "hedge" phrases, such as *likely, may, can, will often,* among many others. When you are being tested on this knowledge, remember that question writers insert these hedge phrases to cover every possibility. Often an answer will be wrong simply because it leaves no room for exception. Extreme positive or negative answers (such as always, never, etc.) are usually not correct. The reader should not use any outside knowledge that is not gathered from the reading passage to answer the related questions. Correct answers can be derived straight from the reading passage.

Literary Genres

Literary genres refer to the basic generic types of poetry, drama, fiction, and nonfiction. Literary genre is a method of classifying and analyzing literature. There are numerous subdivisions within genre, including such categories as novels, novellas, and short stories in fiction. Drama may also be subdivided into comedy, tragedy, and many other categories. Poetry and nonfiction have their own distinct divisions.

Genres often overlap, and the distinctions among them are blurred, such as that between the nonfiction novel and docudrama, as well as many others. However, the use of genres is helpful to the reader as a set of understandings that guide our responses to a work. The generic norm sets expectations and forms the framework within which we read and evaluate a work. This framework will guide both our understanding and interpretation of the work. It is a useful tool for both literary criticism and analysis.

Fiction is a general term for any form of literary narrative that is invented or imagined rather than being factual. For those individuals who equate fact with truth, the imagined or invented character of fiction tends to render it relatively unimportant or trivial among the genres. Defenders of fiction are quick to point out that the fictional mode is an essential part of being. The ability to imagine or discuss what-if plots, characters, and events is clearly part of the human experience.

Prose is derived from the Latin and means "straightforward discourse." Prose fiction, although having many categories, may be divided into three main groups:

- **Short stories**: a fictional narrative, the length of which varies, usually under 20,000 words. Short stories usually have only a few characters and generally describe one major event or insight. The short story began in magazines in the late 1800s and has flourished ever since.
- **Novels**: a longer work of fiction, often containing a large cast of characters and extensive plotting. The emphasis may be on an event, action, social problems, or any experience. There is now a genre of nonfiction novels pioneered by Truman Capote's *In Cold Blood* in the 1960s. Novels may also be written in verse.
- **Novellas**: a work of narrative fiction longer than a short story but shorter than a novel. Novellas may also be called short novels or novelettes. They originated from the German tradition and have become common forms in all of the world's literature.

Many elements influence a work of prose fiction. Some important ones are:

- Speech and dialogue: Characters may speak for themselves or through the narrator. Dialogue may be realistic or fantastic, depending on the author's aim.
- Thoughts and mental processes: There may be internal dialogue used as a device for plot development or character understanding.
- Dramatic involvement: Some narrators encourage readers to become involved in the events of the story, whereas others attempt to distance readers through literary devices.

- Action: This is any information that advances the plot or involves new interactions between the characters.
- Duration: The time frame of the work may be long or short, and the relationship between described time and narrative time may vary.
- Setting and description: Is the setting critical to the plot or characters? How are the action scenes described?
- Themes: This is any point of view or topic given sustained attention.
- Symbolism: Authors often veil meanings through imagery and other literary constructions.

Fiction is much wider than simply prose fiction. Songs, ballads, epics, and narrative poems are examples of non-prose fiction. A full definition of fiction must include not only the work itself but also the framework in which it is read. Literary fiction can also be defined as not true rather than nonexistent, as many works of historical fiction refer to real people, places, and events that are treated imaginatively as if they were true. These imaginary elements enrich and broaden literary expression.

When analyzing fiction, it is important for the reader to look carefully at the work being studied. The plot or action of a narrative can become so entertaining that the language of the work is ignored. The language of fiction should not simply be a way to relate a plot—it should also yield many insights to the judicious reader. Some prose fiction is based on the reader's engagement with the language rather than the story. A studious reader will analyze the mode of expression as well as the narrative. Part of the reward of reading in this manner is to discover how the author uses different language to describe familiar objects, events, or emotions. Some works focus the reader on an author's unorthodox use of language, whereas others may emphasize characters or storylines. What happens in a story is not always the critical element in the work. This type of reading may be difficult at first but yields great rewards.

> **Review Video: Reading Fiction**
> *Visit **mometrix.com/academy** and enter Code:* **391411**

The **narrator** is a central part of any work of fiction, and can give insight about the purpose of the work and its main themes and ideas. The following are important questions to address to better understand the voice and role of the narrator and incorporate that voice into an overall understanding of the novel:

- Who is the narrator of the novel? What is the narrator's perspective, first person or third person? What is the role of the narrator in the plot? Are there changes in narrators or the perspective of narrators?

- Does the narrator explain things in the novel, or does meaning emerge from the plot and events? The personality of the narrator is important. She may have a vested interest in a character or event described. Some narratives follow the time sequence of the plot, whereas others do not. A narrator may express approval or disapproval about a character or events in the work.

- Tone is an important aspect of the narration. Who is actually being addressed by the narrator? Is the tone familiar or formal, intimate or impersonal? Does the vocabulary suggest clues about the narrator?

Review Video: The Narrator
*Visit **mometrix.com/academy** and enter **Code: 742528***

A **character** is a person intimately involved with the plot and development of the novel. Development of the novel's characters not only moves the story along but will also tell the reader a lot about the novel itself. There is usually a physical description of the character, but this is often omitted in modern and postmodern novels. These works may focus on the psychological state or motivation of the character. The choice of a character's name may give valuable clues to his role in the work.

➢ **Review Video: Characters**
*Visit **mometrix.com/academy** and enter **Code: 429493***

Characters are said to be flat or round. Flat characters tend to be minor figures in the story, changing little or not at all. Round characters (those understood from a well-rounded view) are more central to the story and tend to change as the plot unfolds. Stock characters are similar to flat characters, filling out the story without influencing it.

Modern literature has been greatly affected by Freudian psychology, giving rise to such devices as the interior monologue and magical realism as methods of understanding characters in a work. These give the reader a more complex understanding of the inner lives of the characters and enrich the understanding of relationships between characters.

Another important genre is that of **drama**: a play written to be spoken aloud. The drama is in many ways inseparable from performance. Reading drama ideally involves using imagination to visualize and re-create the play with characters and settings. The reader stages the play in his imagination, watching characters interact and developments unfold. Sometimes this involves simulating a theatrical presentation; other times it involves imagining the events. In either case, the reader is imagining the unwritten to re-create the dramatic experience. Novels present some of the same problems, but a narrator will provide much more information about the setting, characters, inner dialogues, and many other supporting details. In drama, much of this is missing, and we are required to use our powers of projection and imagination to taste the full flavor of the dramatic work. There are many empty spaces in dramatic texts that must be filled by the reader to fully appreciate the work.

When reading drama in this way, there are some advantages over watching the play performed (though there is much criticism in this regard):

- Freedom of point of view and perspective: Text is free of interpretations of actors, directors, producers, and technical staging.
- Additional information: The text of a drama may be accompanied by notes or prefaces placing the work in a social or historical context. Stage directions may also provide relevant information about the author's purpose. None of this is typically available at live or filmed performances.
- Study and understanding: Difficult or obscure passages may be studied at leisure and supplemented by explanatory works. This is particularly true of older plays with unfamiliar language, which cannot be fully understood without an opportunity to study the material.

Critical elements of drama, especially when it is being read aloud or performed, include dialect, speech, and dialogue. Analysis of speech and dialogue is important in the critical study of drama. Some playwrights use speech to develop their characters. Speeches may be long or short, and written in as normal prose or blank verse. Some characters have a unique way of speaking which illuminates aspects of the drama. Emphasis and tone are both important, as well. Does the author make clear the tone in which lines are to be spoken, or is this open to interpretation? Sometimes there are various possibilities in tone with regard to delivering lines.

Dialect is any distinct variety of a language, especially one spoken in a region or part of a country. The criterion for distinguishing dialects from languages is that of mutual understanding. For example, people who speak Dutch cannot understand English unless they have learned it. But a speaker from Amsterdam can understand one from Antwerp; therefore, they speak different dialects of the same language. This is, however, a matter of degree; there are languages in which different dialects are unintelligible.

Dialect mixtures are the presence in one form of speech with elements from different neighboring dialects. The study of speech differences from one geographical area to another is called dialect geography. A dialect atlas is a map showing distribution of dialects in a given area. A dialect continuum shows a progressive shift in dialects across a territory, such that adjacent dialects are understandable, but those at the extremes are not.

Dramatic dialogue can be difficult to interpret and changes depending upon the tone used and which words are emphasized. Where the stresses, or meters, of dramatic dialogue fall can determine meaning. Variations in emphasis are only one factor in the manipulability of dramatic speech. Tone is of equal or greater importance and expresses a range of possible emotions and feelings that cannot be readily discerned from the script of a play. The reader must add tone to the words to understand the full meaning of a passage. Recognizing tone is a cumulative process as the reader begins to understand the characters and situations in the play. Other elements that influence the interpretation of dialogue include the setting, possible reactions of the characters to the speech, and possible gestures or facial expressions of the actor. There are no firm rules to guide the interpretation of dramatic speech. An open and flexible attitude is essential in interpreting dramatic dialogue.

Action is a crucial element in the production of a dramatic work. Many dramas contain little dialogue and much action. In these cases, it is essential for the reader to carefully study stage directions and visualize the action on the stage. Benefits of understanding stage directions include knowing which characters are on the stage at all times, who is speaking to whom, and following these patterns through changes of scene.

Stage directions also provide additional information, some of which is not available to a live audience. The nature of the physical space where the action occurs is vital, and stage directions help with this. The historical context of the period is important in understanding what the playwright was working with in terms of theaters and physical space. The type of staging possible for the author is a good guide to the spatial elements of a production.

> ➤ **Review Video: Action and Stage Directions**
> Visit **mometrix.com/academy** and enter **Code: 539974**

Asides and soliloquies are devices that authors use in plot and character development. **Asides** indicate that not all characters are privy to the lines. This may be a method of advancing or explaining the plot in a subtle manner. **Soliloquies** are opportunities for character development, plot enhancement, and to give insight to characters motives, feelings, and emotions. Careful study of these elements provides a reader with an abundance of clues to the major themes and plot of the work.

Art, music, and literature all interact in ways that contain many opportunities for the enrichment of all of the arts. Students could apply their knowledge of art and music by creating illustrations for a work or creating a musical score for a text. Students could discuss the meanings of texts and decide on their illustrations, or a score could amplify the meaning of the text.

Understanding the art and music of a period can make the experience of literature a richer, more rewarding experience. Students should be encouraged to use the knowledge of art and music to illuminate the text. Examining examples of dress, architecture, music, and dance of a period may be helpful in a fuller engagement of the text. Much of period literature lends itself to the analysis of the prevailing taste in art and music of an era, which helps place the literary work in a more meaningful context.

Critical Thinking Skills

Opinions, Facts, & Fallacies

Critical thinking skills are mastered through understanding various types of writing and the different purposes that authors have for writing the way they do. Every author writes for a purpose. Understanding that purpose, and how they accomplish their goal, will allow you to critique the writing and determine whether or not you agree with their conclusions.

Readers must always be conscious of the distinction between fact and opinion. A **fact** can be subjected to analysis and can be either proved or disproved. An **opinion**, on the other hand, is the author's personal feeling, which may not be alterable by research, evidence, or argument. If the author writes that the distance from New York to Boston is about two hundred miles, he is stating a fact. But if he writes that New York is too crowded, then he is giving an opinion, because there is no objective standard for overpopulation. An opinion may be indicated by words like *believe, think,* or *feel*. Also, an opinion may be supported by facts: for instance, the author might give the population density of New York as a reason for why it is overcrowded. An opinion supported by fact tends to be more convincing. When authors support their opinions with other opinions, the reader is unlikely to be moved.

Facts should be presented to the reader from reliable sources. An opinion is what the author thinks about a given topic. An opinion is not common knowledge or proven by expert sources, but it is information that the author believes and wants the reader to consider. To distinguish between fact and opinion, a reader needs to look at the type of source that is presenting information, what information backs-up a claim, and whether or not the author may be motivated to have a certain point of view on a given topic. For example, if a panel of scientists has conducted multiple studies on the effectiveness of taking a certain vitamin, the results are more likely to be factual than if a company selling a vitamin claims that taking the vitamin can produce positive effects. The company is motivated to sell its product, while the scientists are using the scientific method to prove a theory. If the author uses words such as "I think…", the statement is an opinion.

> ➤ **Review Video:** <u>Fact or Opinion</u>
> *Visit **mometrix.com/academy** and enter **Code: 870899***

In their attempt to persuade, writers often make mistakes in their thinking patterns and writing choices. It's important to understand these so you can make an informed decision. Every author has a point of view, but when an author ignores reasonable counterarguments or distorts opposing viewpoints, she is demonstrating a **bias**. A bias is evident whenever the author is unfair or inaccurate in his or her presentation. Bias may be intentional or unintentional, but it should always alert the reader to be skeptical of the argument being made. It should be noted that a biased author may still be correct. However, the author will be correct in spite of her bias, not because of it.

A **stereotype** is like a bias, except that it is specifically applied to a group or place. Stereotyping is considered to be particularly abhorrent because it promotes negative generalizations about people. Many people are familiar with some of the hateful stereotypes of certain ethnic, religious, and cultural groups. Readers should be very wary of authors who stereotype. These faulty assumptions typically reveal the author's ignorance and lack of curiosity.

> ➤ **Review Video:** <u>Bias and Stereotype</u>
> *Visit **mometrix.com/academy** and enter **Code: 644829***

Sometimes, authors will **appeal to the reader's emotions** in an attempt to persuade or to distract the reader from the weakness of the argument. For instance, the author may try to inspire the pity of the reader by delivering a heart-rending story.

> ➤ **Review Video:** <u>Appeal to the Reader's Emotions</u>
> *Visit **mometrix.com/academy** and enter **Code: 163442***

An author also might use the bandwagon approach, in which he suggests that his opinion is correct because it is held by the majority. Some authors resort to name-calling, in which insults and harsh words are delivered to the opponent in an attempt to distract. In advertising, a common appeal is the testimonial, in which a famous person endorses a product. Of course, the fact that a celebrity likes something should not really mean anything to the reader. These and other emotional appeals are usually evidence of poor reasoning and a weak argument.

Certain *logical fallacies* are frequent in writing. A logical fallacy is a failure of reasoning. As a reader, it is important to recognize logical fallacies, because they diminish the value of the author's message. The four most common logical fallacies in writing are the false analogy, circular reasoning, false dichotomy, and overgeneralization. In a **false analogy**, the author suggests that two things are similar, when in fact they are different. This fallacy is often committed when the author is attempting to convince the reader that something unknown is like something relatively familiar. The author takes advantage of the reader's ignorance to make this false comparison. One example might be the following statement: *Failing to tip a waitress is like stealing money out of somebody's wallet*. Of course, failing to tip is very rude, especially when the service has been good, but people are not arrested for failing to tip as they would for stealing money from a wallet. To compare stingy diners with thieves is a false analogy.

> ➤ **Review Video:** <u>False Analogy</u>
> *Visit **mometrix.com/academy** and enter **Code: 865045***

Circular reasoning is one of the more difficult logical fallacies to identify, because it is typically hidden behind dense language and complicated sentences. Reasoning is described as circular when it offers no support for assertions other than restating them in different words. Put another way, a circular argument refers to itself as evidence of truth. A simple example of circular argument is when a person uses a word to define itself, such as saying *Niceness is the state of being nice*. If the reader does not know what *nice* means, then this definition will not be very useful. In a text, circular reasoning is usually more complex. For instance, an author might say *Poverty is a problem for society because it creates trouble for people throughout the community*. It is redundant to say that poverty is a problem because it creates trouble. When an author engages in circular reasoning, it is often because he or she has not fully thought out the argument, or cannot come up with any legitimate justifications.

> ➤ **Review Video:** <u>Circular Reasoning</u>
> *Visit **mometrix.com/academy** and enter **Code: 398925***

One of the most common logical fallacies is the **false dichotomy**, in which the author creates an artificial sense that there are only two possible alternatives in a situation. This fallacy is common when the author has an agenda and wants to give the impression that his view is the only sensible one. A false dichotomy has the effect of limiting the reader's options and imagination. An example of a false dichotomy is the statement *You need to go to the party with me, otherwise you'll just be bored at home.* The speaker suggests that the only other possibility besides being at the party is being bored at home. But this is not true, as it is perfectly possible to be entertained at home, or even to go somewhere other than the party. Readers should always be wary of the false dichotomy: when an author limits alternatives, it is always wise to ask whether he is being valid.

> ➤ **Review Video:** <u>False Dichotomy</u>
> *Visit **mometrix.com/academy** and enter **Code:** **484397***

Overgeneralization is a logical fallacy in which the author makes a claim that is so broad it cannot be proved or disproved. In most cases, overgeneralization occurs when the author wants to create an illusion of authority, or when he is using sensational language to sway the opinion of the reader. For instance, in the sentence *Everybody knows that she is a terrible teacher*, the author makes an assumption that cannot really be believed. This kind of statement is made when the author wants to create the illusion of consensus when none actually exists: it may be that most people have a negative view of the teacher, but to say that *everybody* feels that way is an exaggeration. When a reader spots overgeneralization, she should become skeptical about the argument that is being made, because an author will often try to hide a weak or unsupported assertion behind authoritative language.

> ➤ **Review Video:** <u>Overgeneralization</u>
> *Visit **mometrix.com/academy** and enter **Code:** **367357***

Two other types of logical fallacies are **slippery slope** arguments and **hasty generalizations**. In a slippery slope argument, the author says that if something happens, it automatically means that something else will happen as a result, even though this may not be true. (i.e., just because you study hard does not mean you are going to ace the test). "Hasty generalization" is drawing a conclusion too early, without finishing analyzing the details of the argument. Writers of persuasive texts often use these techniques because they are very effective. In order to **identify logical fallacies**, readers need to read carefully and ask questions as they read. Thinking critically means not taking everything at face value. Readers need to critically evaluate an author's argument to make sure that the logic used is sound.

Organization of the Text

The way a text is organized can help the reader to understand more clearly the author's intent and his conclusions. There are various ways to organize a text, and each one has its own purposes and uses.

Some nonfiction texts are organized to **present a problem** followed by a solution. In this type of text, it is common for the problem to be explained before the solution is offered. In some cases, as when the problem is well known, the solution may be briefly introduced at the beginning. The entire passage may focus on the solution, and the problem will be referenced only occasionally. Some texts will outline multiple solutions to a problem, leaving the reader to choose among them. If the author has an interest or an allegiance to one solution, he may fail to mention or may describe inaccurately some of the other solutions. Readers should be careful of the author's agenda when reading a problem-solution text. Only by understanding the author's point of view and interests can one develop a proper judgment of the proposed solution.

Authors need to organize information logically so the reader can follow it and locate information within the text. Two common organizational structures are cause and effect and chronological order. When using **chronological order**, the author presents information in the order that it happened. For example, biographies are written in chronological order; the subject's birth and childhood are presented first, followed by their adult life, and lastly by the events leading up to the person's death.

In **cause and effect**, an author presents one thing that makes something else happen. For example, if one were to go to bed very late, they would be tired. The cause is going to bed late, with the effect of being tired the next day.

It can be tricky to identify the cause-and-effect relationships in a text, but there are a few ways to approach this task. To begin with, these relationships are often signaled with certain terms. When an author uses words like *because*, *since*, *in order*, and *so*, she is likely describing a cause-and-effect relationship. Consider the sentence, "He called her because he needed the homework." This is a simple causal relationship, in which the cause was his need for the homework and the effect was his phone call. Not all cause-and-effect relationships are marked in this way, however. Consider the sentences, "He called her. He needed the homework." When the cause-and-effect relationship is not indicated with a keyword, it can be discovered by asking why something happened. He called her: why? The answer is in the next sentence: He needed the homework.

Persuasive essays, in which an author tries to make a convincing argument and change the reader's mind, usually include cause-and-effect relationships. However, these relationships should not always be taken at face value. An author frequently will assume a cause or take an effect for granted. To read a persuasive essay effectively, one needs to judge the cause-and-effect relationships the author is presenting. For instance, imagine an author wrote the following: "The parking deck has been unprofitable because people would prefer to ride their bikes." The relationship is clear: the cause is that people prefer to ride their bikes, and the effect is that the parking deck has been unprofitable. However, a reader should consider whether this argument is conclusive. Perhaps there are other reasons for the failure of the parking deck: a down economy, excessive fees, etc. Too often, authors present causal relationships as if they are fact rather than opinion. Readers should be on the alert for these dubious claims.

Thinking critically about ideas and conclusions can seem like a daunting task. One way to make it easier is to understand the basic elements of ideas and writing techniques. Looking at the way different ideas relate to each other can be a good way for the reader to begin his analysis. For instance, sometimes writers will write about two different ideas that are in opposition to each other. The analysis of these opposing ideas is known as **contrast**. Contrast is often marred by the author's obvious partiality to one of the ideas. A discerning reader will be put off by an author who does not engage in a fair fight. In an analysis of opposing ideas, both ideas should be presented in their clearest and most reasonable terms.

If the author does prefer a side, he should avoid indicating this preference with pejorative language. An analysis of opposing ideas should proceed through the major differences point by point, with a full explanation of each side's view. For instance, in an analysis of capitalism and communism, it would be important to outline each side's view on labor, markets, prices, personal responsibility, etc. It would be less effective to describe the theory of communism and then explain how capitalism has thrived in the West. An analysis of opposing views should present each side in the same manner.

Many texts follow the **compare-and-contrast** model, in which the similarities and differences between two ideas or things are explored. Analysis of the similarities between ideas is called comparison. In order for a comparison to work, the author must place the ideas or things in an equivalent structure. That is, the author must present the ideas in the same way.

Imagine an author wanted to show the similarities between cricket and baseball. The correct way to do so would be to summarize the equipment and rules for each game. It would be incorrect to summarize the equipment of cricket and then lay out the history of baseball, since this would make it impossible for the reader to see the similarities. It is perhaps too obvious to say that an analysis of similar ideas should emphasize the similarities. Of course, the author should take care to include any differences that must be mentioned. Often, these small differences will only reinforce the more general similarity.

> **Review Video: <u>Strategy of Comparing and Contrasting</u>**
> *Visit **mometrix.com/academy** and enter **Code: 587299***

Drawing Conclusions

Authors should have a clear purpose in mind while writing. Especially when reading informational texts, it is important to understand the logical conclusion of the author's ideas. **Identifying this logical conclusion** can help the reader understand whether he agrees with the writer or not. Identifying a logical conclusion is much like making an inference: it requires the reader to combine the information given by the text with what he already knows to make a supportable assertion. If a passage is written well, then the conclusion should be obvious even when it is unstated. If the author intends the reader to draw a certain conclusion, then all of his argumentation and detail should be leading toward it. One way to approach the task of drawing conclusions is to make brief notes of all the points made by the author. When these are arranged on paper, they may clarify the logical conclusion. Another way to approach conclusions is to consider whether the reasoning of the author raises any pertinent questions. Sometimes it will be possible to draw several conclusions from a passage, and on occasion these will be conclusions that were never imagined by the author. It is essential, however, that these conclusions be supported directly by the text.

The term **text evidence** refers to information that supports a main point or points in a story, and can help lead the reader to a conclusion. Information used as *text evidence* is precise, descriptive, and factual. A main point is often followed by supporting details that provide evidence to back-up a claim. For example, a story may include the claim that winter occurs during opposite months in the Northern and Southern hemispheres. *Text evidence* based on this claim may include countries where winter occurs in opposite months, along with reasons that winter occurs at different times of the year in separate hemispheres (due to the tilt of the Earth as it rotates around the sun).

Readers interpret text and respond to it in a number of ways. Using textual support helps defend your response or interpretation because it roots your thinking in the text. You are interpreting based on information in the text and not simply your own ideas. When crafting a response, look for important quotes and details from the text to help bolster your argument. If you are writing about a character's personality trait, for example, use details from the text to show that the character acted in such a way. You can also include statistics and facts from a nonfiction text to strengthen your response. For example, instead of writing, "A lot of people use cell phones," use statistics to provide the exact number. This strengthens your argument because it is more precise.

The text used to support an argument can be the argument's downfall if it is not credible. A text is **credible**, or believable, when the author is knowledgeable and objective, or unbiased. The author's motivations for writing the text play a critical role in determining the credibility of the text and must be evaluated when assessing that credibility. The author's motives should be for the dissemination of information. The purpose of the text should be to inform or describe, not to persuade. When an author writes a persuasive text, he has the motivation that the reader will do what they want. The extent of the author's knowledge of the topic and their motivation must be evaluated when assessing the credibility of a text. Reports written about the Ozone layer by an environmental scientist and a hairdresser will have a different level of credibility.

After determining your own opinion and evaluating the credibility of your supporting text, it is sometimes necessary to communicate your ideas and findings to others. When **writing a response to a text**, it is important to use elements of the text to support your assertion or defend your position. Using supporting evidence from the text strengthens the argument because the reader can see how in depth the writer read the original piece and based their response on the details and facts within that text. Elements of text that can be used in a response include: facts, details, statistics, and direct quotations from the text. When writing a response, one must make sure they indicate which information comes from the original text and then base their discussion, argument, or defense around this information.

A reader should always be drawing conclusions from the text. Sometimes conclusions are implied from written information, and other times the information is **stated directly** within the passage. It is always more comfortable to draw conclusions from information stated within a passage, rather than to draw them from mere implications. At times an author may provide some information and then describe a counterargument. The reader should be alert for direct statements that are subsequently rejected or weakened by the author. The reader should always read the entire passage before drawing conclusions. Many readers are trained to expect the author's conclusions at either the beginning or the end of the passage, but many texts do not adhere to this format.

Drawing conclusions from information implied within a passage requires confidence on the part of the reader. **Implications** are things the author does not state directly, but which can be assumed based on what the author does say. For instance, consider the following simple passage: "I stepped outside and opened my umbrella. By the time I got to work, the cuffs of my pants were soaked." The author never states that it is raining, but this fact is clearly implied. Conclusions based on implication must be well supported by the text. In order to draw a solid conclusion, a reader should have multiple pieces of evidence, or, if he only has one, must be assured that there is no other possible explanation than his conclusion. A good reader will be able to draw many conclusions from information implied by the text, which enriches the reading experience considerably.

As an aid to drawing conclusions, the reader should be adept at **outlining** the information contained in the passage; an effective outline will reveal the structure of the passage, and will lead to solid conclusions. An effective outline will have a title that refers to the basic subject of the text, though it need not recapitulate the main idea. In most outlines, the main idea will be the first major section. It will have each major idea of the passage established as the head of a category. For instance, the most common outline format calls for the main ideas of the passage to be indicated with Roman numerals. In an effective outline of this kind, each of the main ideas will be represented by a Roman numeral and none of the Roman numerals will designate minor details or secondary ideas. Moreover, all supporting ideas and details should be placed in the appropriate place on the outline. An outline does not need to include every detail listed in the text, but it should feature all of those that are central to the argument or message. Each of these details should be listed under the appropriate main idea.

It is also helpful to **summarize** the information you have read in a paragraph or passage format. This process is similar to creating an effective outline. To begin with, a summary should accurately define the main idea of the passage, though it does not need to explain this main idea in exhaustive detail. It should continue by laying out the most important supporting details or arguments from the passage. All of the significant supporting details should be included, and none of the details included should be irrelevant or insignificant. Also, the summary should accurately report all of these details. Too often, the desire for brevity in a summary leads to the sacrifice of clarity or veracity. Summaries are often difficult to read, because they omit all of graceful language, digressions, and asides that distinguish great writing. However, if the summary is effective, it should contain much the same message as the original text.

Paraphrasing is another method the reader can use to aid in comprehension. When paraphrasing, one puts what they have read into their own words, rephrasing what the author has written to make it their own, to "translate" all of what the author says to their own words, including as many details as they can.

Testing Tips

Question scanning

On standardized tests, the reading comprehension section will generally contain a paragraph followed by a series of questions. Students may find it helpful to read each of the questions before reading the paragraph. This will alert them to the specific details they should look for while reading. Then, as they read the paragraph, students will find that the answers to the questions will be more obvious. Scanning questions before reading can also provide a basic idea of what the content of the paragraph will be. For example, if all of the questions deal with pacemakers, students can expect an article about that topic. Students should also pay attention to the nature of the questions, such as whether they are general or specific. Questions that ask for names or dates might indicate that students should jot down names and dates as they read the passage. For answers that do not readily appear in the course of reading, students should reread the questions and carefully consider each possible answer choice.

Skimming

Your first task when you begin reading is to answer the question "What is the topic of the selection?" This can best be answered by quickly skimming the passage for the general idea, stopping to read only the first sentence of each paragraph. A paragraph's first sentence is usually the main topic sentence, and it gives you a summary of the content of the paragraph.

Once you've skimmed the passage, stopping to read only the first sentences, you will have a general idea about what it is about, as well as what is the expected topic in each paragraph.

Each question will contain clues as to where to find the answer in the passage. Do not just randomly search through the passage for the correct answer to each question. Search scientifically. Find key word(s) or ideas in the question that are going to either contain or be near the correct answer. These are typically nouns, verbs, numbers, or phrases in the question that will probably be duplicated in the passage. Once you have identified those key word(s) or idea, skim the passage quickly to find where those key word(s) or idea appears. The correct answer choice will be nearby.

Example: What caused Martin to suddenly return to Paris?

The key word is Paris. Skim the passage quickly to find where this word appears. The answer will be close by that word. However, sometimes key words in the question are not repeated in the passage. In those cases, search for the general idea of the question.

Example: Which of the following was the psychological impact of the author's childhood upon the remainder of his life?

Key words are "childhood" or "psychology". While searching for those words, be alert for other words or phrases that have similar meaning, such as "emotional effect" or "mentally" which could be used in the passage, rather than the exact word "psychology". Numbers or years can be particularly good key words to skim for, as they stand out from the rest of the text.

Example: Which of the following best describes the influence of Monet's work in the 20th century?

20th contains numbers and will easily stand out from the rest of the text. Use 20th as the key word to skim for in the passage. Other good key word(s) may be in quotation marks. These identify a word or phrase that is copied directly from the passage. In those cases, the word(s) in quotation marks are exactly duplicated in the passage.

Example: In her college years, what was meant by Margaret's "drive for excellence"?

"Drive for excellence" is a direct quote from the passage and should be easy to find.

Once you've quickly found the correct section of the passage to find the answer, focus upon the answer choices. Sometimes a choice will repeat word for word a portion of the passage near the answer. However, beware of such duplication – it may be a trap! More than likely, the correct choice will paraphrase or summarize the related portion of the passage, rather than being exactly the same wording.

For the answers that you think are correct, read them carefully and make sure that they answer the question. An answer can be factually correct, but it MUST answer the question asked. Additionally, two answers can both be seemingly correct, so be sure to read all of the answer choices, and make sure that you get the one that BEST answers the question. Some questions will not have a key word.

Example: Which of the following would the author of this passage likely agree with?

In these cases, look for key words in the answer choices. Then skim the passage to find where the answer choice occurs. By skimming to find where to look, you can minimize the time required.

Sometimes it may be difficult to identify a good key word in the question to skim for in the passage. In those cases, look for a key word in one of the answer choices to skim for. Often the answer choices can all be found in the same paragraph, which can quickly narrow your search.

Summarizing a passage

Summarizing a passage can seem like an overwhelming task, especially when it is a long passage. However, summarizing can help students understand the main idea of a passage, as well as the writer's tone and purpose. Summarizing a passage is a skill that must be practiced. Students should follow three basic rules when summarizing. First, they should list the main ideas from the beginning, middle, and end of the passage. Second, they should always summarize in sequence. In other words, they should not skip around in the passage, but should summarize from beginning to middle to end. Third, students should make sure that the summary contains accurate information. Test questions may ask students to select the best summary of a passage. By using these three rules, students will be able to eliminate incorrect answers and select the best answer.

Paragraph focus

Focus upon the first sentence of each paragraph, which is the most important. The main topic of the paragraph is usually there.

Once you've read the first sentence in the paragraph, you have a general idea about what each paragraph will be about. As you read the questions, try to determine which paragraph will have the answer. Paragraphs have a concise topic. The answer should either obviously be there or obviously not. It will save time if you can jump straight to the paragraph, so try to remember what you learned from the first sentences.
Example: The first paragraph is about poets; the second is about poetry. If a question asks about poetry, where will the answer be? *The second paragraph.*

The main idea of a passage is typically spread across all or most of its paragraphs. Whereas the main idea of a paragraph may be completely different than the main idea of the very next paragraph, a main idea for a passage affects all of the paragraphs in one form or another.
Example: What is the main idea of the passage?

For each answer choice, try to see how many paragraphs are related. It can help to count how many sentences are affected by each choice, but it is best to see how many paragraphs are affected by the choice. Typically the answer choices will include incorrect choices that are main ideas of individual paragraphs, but not the entire passage. That is why it is crucial to choose ideas that are supported by the most paragraphs possible.

Main idea of a passage

A paragraph contains a group of connected sentences. Each sentence of a paragraph relates to the paragraph's main idea. The main idea is the central theme or topic of a paragraph or larger text. A writer uses a main idea to organize the text. Identifying the main idea will help the reader understand the passage being read. Main ideas can be found anywhere in a passage. Often, a passage may appear to contain several main ideas, but careful reading will reveal that one idea is more important than the others. A main idea is an important concept for both writers and readers.

The student has found the main idea of a passage when he or she understands the point that the writer is attempting to make. To accomplish this, the student must be able to read a short or long passage and then distill the information into a single idea. The student should start by reviewing the passage and finding the main idea of each paragraph. Once the main idea of each paragraph is identified, the student should be able to recognize a recurring or cohesive theme. However, if a test question asks a student to select the main idea of a passage from four possible answer choices and the student is unsure of the correct answer, the student can count the number of paragraphs in which each answer choice is mentioned. The choice that is mentioned in most of the paragraphs is usually the correct answer.

Questions pertaining to view, inference, and definitions

Test questions may be multiple-choice or open-ended. Students will be asked to read a narrative passage and then answer a series of questions. Questions that concern the story's point of view will refer to the perspective from which the story is told or to the way a character feels about an event, a setting, or another character. Inference questions will ask students to determine the meaning of a group of words from the narrative. Often these phrases will use figurative language such as a simile or a metaphor. Definition questions will require students to determine the meaning of a word used in the narrative.

Questions pertaining to descriptions, tone, and themes

Test questions may be multiple-choice or open-ended. Students will be asked to read a narrative passage and then answer a series of questions. Some questions may ask students to select a word or phrase that best describes an element of the story, or they may ask students to describe a setting, character, or event. Other questions may ask students to answer questions regarding the tone of the story. Tone can include a range of emotions, including sadness, hope, and excitement. The tone depends on the overall feeling of the narrative as created by the writer or narrator. Questions may also address themes within a narrative, such as loss, love, conflict, or fear.

Questions pertaining to key events and general reading knowledge

Test questions may be multiple-choice or open-ended. Students will be asked to read a narrative passage and then answer a series of questions. Some questions may address key events that occur in the narrative. Students must be able to identify turning points, climaxes, and resolutions in a story. Students must also be able to recognize the point in a story where a character makes an important decision or undergoes a dramatic change. Questions that test general reading knowledge may ask students to use real-life experience to relate to a narrative. For example, students may be asked what type of life experience would best aid one in understanding the motives of a character in a story about a teenager who runs away from home.

Main point or fact vs. opinion questions

Students will be asked to read a given passage and then answer a series of questions. One type of question that students may encounter is a main point question. Such a question will ask, "Which of the following sentences best describes the main point of the passage?" Students must be able to determine which of the answer choices provided is most likely to represent the main idea of the passage. Another type of question that students may encounter is a fact versus opinion question. In this type of question, students are given a statement and must determine if it is a fact or an opinion. Distinguishing between fact and opinion is an important skill to master when reading a persuasive text.

Questions pertaining to writer's argument, persuasive methods, and perspective

Students will be asked to read a given passage and then answer a series of questions. Some questions may ask students to select an answer that supports the writer's main argument. Students may also be asked to select an answer that undermines that argument. Other questions may require the student to identify the method or methods of persuasion used in a passage. Persuasive methods can include exaggeration, emotional appeal, or authoritative appeal. Students should be able to read two passages and compare and contrast the writers' ideas from the two passages. Questions concerning the authors' perspectives may ask students to choose a statement with which both writers would most likely agree.

Purpose and tone

Readers and writers perform their tasks with the same purposes. Writers write to inform or to entertain; readers read to be informed or to be entertained. A writer may sometimes, however, present an entertaining piece of writing as an informative piece, or a writer may attempt to manipulate readers by presenting an opinion as an objective statement. Readers must be able to distinguish a writer's purpose and tone in order to fully comprehend the writer's intent. A reader should ask two questions: 1) Who is the audience? and 2) Why is this being written? A writer may be attempting to persuade the reader to act on something or to think a certain way. A passage that contains words with either positive or negative connotations usually indicates that the writer is attempting to persuade a reader.

Fact and opinion

A successful reader is able to interpret a writer's intent. For instance, writers express many of their own values, opinions, and beliefs in their writing. Readers must distinguish between the facts and opinions presented by a writer. A fact is a piece of information that can be proven, while an opinion is simply one person's view or belief. Opinions cannot be proven. A fact is objective, while an opinion is subjective. Concrete, measurable words often indicate a factual piece of information. Opinions are often presented with judgmental or emotional terms, such as *best, worst, easiest*, and *ugliest*, that indicate the statement is an opinion.

When asked about which statement is a fact or opinion, remember that answer choices that are facts will typically have no ambiguous words. For example, how long is a long time? What defines an ordinary person? These ambiguous words of "long" and "ordinary" should not be in a factual statement. However, if all of the choices have ambiguous words, go to the context of the passage. Often a factual statement may be set out as a research finding. *Example*:

"The scientist found that the eye reacts quickly to change in light."

Opinions may be set out in the context of words like thought, believed, understood, or wished.

Example:

"He thought the Yankees should win the World Series."

Logical inferences

Inferences are educated guesses that can be drawn from the facts and information available to a reader. Inferences are usually based on a reader's own assumptions and beliefs. The ability to make inferences is often called "reading between the lines." There are three basic types of inferences: deductive reasoning, abductive reasoning, and inductive reasoning. Deductive reasoning is the ability to find an effect when given a cause and a rule. Abductive reasoning is the ability to find a cause when given a rule and an effect. Inductive reasoning is the ability to find a rule when given a cause and an effect. Each type of reasoning can be used to make logical inferences from a text.

Opposites

Answer choices that are direct opposites are usually correct. The paragraph will often contain established relationships (when this goes up, that goes down). The question may ask you to draw conclusions for this and will give two similar answer choices that are opposites.

Example:

A. if other factors are held constant, then increasing the interest rate will lead to a decrease in housing starts

B. if other factors are held constant, then increasing the interest rate will lead to an increase in housing starts

Often these opposites will not be so clearly recognized. Don't be thrown off by different wording, look for the meaning beneath. Notice how these two answer choices are really opposites, with just a slight change in the wording shown above. Once you realize these are opposites, you should examine them closely. One of these two is likely to be the correct answer.

Example:

    A. if other factors are held constant, then increasing the interest rate will lead to a decrease in housing starts

    B. when there is an increase in housing starts, and other things remaining equal, it is often the result of an increase in interest rates

Word usage questions

When asked how a word is used in the passage, don't use your existing knowledge of the word. The question is being asked precisely because there is some strange or unusual usage of the word in the passage. Go to the passage and use contextual clues to determine the answer. Don't simply use the popular definition you already know.

Eliminate Choices

Some choices can quickly be eliminated. "Andy Warhol lived there." Is Andy Warhol even mentioned in the article? If not, quickly eliminate it. When trying to answer a question such as "the passage indicates all of the following EXCEPT" quickly skim the paragraph searching for references to each choice. If the reference exists, scratch it off as a choice. Similar choices may be crossed off simultaneously if they are close enough.

In choices that ask you to choose "which answer choice does NOT describe?" or "all of the following answer choices are identifiable characteristics, EXCEPT which?" look for answers that are similarly worded. Since only one answer can be correct, if there are two answers that appear to mean the same thing, they must BOTH be incorrect, and can be eliminated.

Example:

    A. changing values and attitudes

    B. a large population of mobile or uprooted people

These answer choices are similar; they both describe a fluid culture. Because of their similarity, they can be linked together. Since the answer can have only one choice, they can also be eliminated together.

Writing

Brainstorm

Spend the first few minutes brainstorming out ideas. Write down any ideas you might have on the topic. The purpose is to extract from the recesses of your memory any relevant information. In this stage, anything goes down. Write down any idea, regardless of how good it may initially seem.

Creating a thesis

The topic should be clear and easily understood by readers. The writer should explain, using reliable and current data gathered through research, why readers should care about the selected topic. It may be helpful for the writer to find published arguments that relate to the topic or idea. These arguments can help to the writer evaluate his or her own techniques and information. Finally, the writer should make certain that all of the elements he or she plans to use do in fact support the claim.

Diversity

The best papers will contain diversity of examples and reasoning. As you brainstorm consider different perspectives. Not only are there two sides to every issue, but there are also countless perspectives that can be considered. On any issue, different groups are impacted, with many reaching the same conclusion or position, but through vastly different paths. Try to "see" the issue through as many different eyes as you can. Look at it from every angle and from every vantage point. The more diverse the reasoning used, the more balanced the paper will become and the better the score.

Example:

The issue of free trade is not just two sided. It impacts politicians, domestic (US) manufacturers, foreign manufacturers, the US economy, the world economy, strategic alliances, retailers, wholesalers, consumers, unions, workers, and the exchange of more than just goods, but also of ideas, beliefs, and cultures. The more of these angles that you can approach the issue from, the more solid your reasoning and the stronger your position.

Furthermore, don't just use information as to how the issue impacts other people. Draw liberally from your own experience and your own observations. Explain a personal experience that you have had and your own emotions from that moment. Anything that you've seen in your community or observed in society can be expanded upon to further round out your position on the issue.

Main idea

Once you have finished with your creative flow, stop and review it. Which idea were you able to come up with the most supporting information? It's extremely important that you pick an angle that will allow you to have a thorough and comprehensive coverage of the topic. This is not about your personal convictions, but about writing a concise rational discussion of an idea.

Strong points

Every garden of ideas gets weeds in it. The ideas that you brainstormed over are going to be random pieces of information of mixed value. Go through it methodically and pick out the ones that are the best. The best ideas are strong points that it will be easy to write a few sentences or a paragraph about.

Logical flow

Now that you know which ideas you are going to use and focus upon, organize them. Put your writing points in a logical order. You have your main ideas that you will focus on, and must align them in a sequence that will flow in a smooth, sensible path from point to point, so that the reader will go smoothly from one idea to the next in a logical path. Readers must have a sense of continuity as they read your paper. You don't want to have a paper that rambles back and forth.

Expand on ideas

You have a logical flow of main ideas with which to start writing. Begin expanding on the issues in the sequence that you have set for yourself. Pace yourself. Don't spend too much time on any one of the ideas that you are expanding upon. You want to have time for all of them. Make sure you watch your time. If you have twenty minutes left to write out your ideas and you have ten ideas, then you can only use two minutes per idea. It can be a daunting task to cram a lot of information down in words in a short amount of time, but if you pace yourself, you can get through it all. If you find that you are falling behind, speed up. Move through each idea more quickly, spending less time to expand upon the idea in order to catch back up.

Once you finish expanding on each idea, go back to your brainstorming session up above, where you wrote out your ideas. Go ahead and erase the ideas as you write about them. This will let you see what you need to write about next, and also allow you to pace yourself and see what you have left to cover.

First paragraph

Your first paragraph should have several easily identifiable features.

First, it should have a quick description or paraphrasing of the topic. Use your own words to briefly explain what the topic is about.

Second, you should explain your opinion of the topic and give an explanation of why you feel that way. What is your decision or conclusion on the topic?

Third, you should list your "writing points". What are the main ideas that you came up with earlier? This is your opportunity to outline the rest of your paper. Have a sentence explaining each idea that you will go intend further depth in additional paragraphs. If someone was to only read this paragraph, they should be able to get an "executive summary" of the entire paper.

Body paragraph

Each of your successive paragraphs should expand upon one of the points listed in the main paragraph. Use your personal experience and knowledge to support each of your points. Examples should back up everything.

Conclusion paragraph

Once you have finished expanding upon each of your main points, wrap it up. Summarize what you have said and covered in a conclusion paragraph. Explain once more your opinion of the topic and quickly review why you feel that way. At this stage, you have already backed up your statements, so there is no need to do that again. All you are doing is refreshing in the mind of the reader the main points that you have made.

Transitional words and phrases

Transitional words and phrases are used to transition between paragraphs and also to transition within a single paragraph. Transitions assist the flow of ideas and help to unify an essay. When a writer links ideas that are similar in nature, there are a variety of words and phrases he or she can choose, including but not limited to: *also, and, another, besides, equally important, further, furthermore, in addition, likewise, too, similarly, nor, of course*, and *for instance*. Writers can link contradictory ideas in an essay by using, among others, the following words and phrases: *although, and yet, even if, conversely, but, however, otherwise, still, yet, instead, in spite of, nevertheless, on the contrary*, and *on the other hand*.

Writers may need to indicate that one thing is the cause, purpose, or result of another thing. To show this relationship, writers can use, among others, the following linking words and phrases: *as, as a result, because, consequently, hence, for, for this reason, since, so, then, thus*, and *therefore*. Certain words can be used to indicate the time and position of one thing in relation to another. Writers can use, for example, the following terms to create a timeline of events in an essay: *above, across, afterward, before, beyond, eventually, meanwhile, next, presently, around, at once, at the present time, finally, first, here, second, thereafter*, and *upon*. These words can show the order or placement of items or ideas in an essay.

A writer can use certain words to indicate that an example or summary is being presented. The following phrases, among others, can be used as this type of transition: *as a result, as I have said, for example, for instance, in any case, in any event, in brief, in conclusion, in fact, in other words, in short, on the whole,* and *to sum it up.*

Don't panic

Panicking will not put down any more words on paper for you. Therefore, it isn't helpful. When you first see the topic, if your mind goes as blank as the page on which you have to write out your paper, take a deep breath. Force yourself to mechanically go through the steps listed above.

Secondly, don't get clock fever. It's easy to be overwhelmed when you're looking at a page that doesn't seem to have much text, there is a lot of blank space further down, your mind is full of random thoughts and feeling confused, and the clock is ticking down faster than you would like. You brainstormed first so that you don't have to keep coming up with ideas. If you're running out of time and you have a lot of ideas that you haven't expanded upon, don't be afraid to make some cuts. Start picking the best ideas that you have left and expand on those few. Don't feel like you have to write down and expand all of your ideas.

Check your work

It is more important to have a shorter paper that is well written and well organized, than a longer paper that is poorly written and poorly organized. Don't keep writing about a subject just to add words and sentences, and certainly don't start repeating yourself. Expand on the ideas that you identified in the brainstorming session and make sure that you save yourself a few minutes at the end to go back and check your work.

Leave time at the end, at least a few minutes, to go back and check over your work. Reread and make sure that everything you've written makes sense and flows. Clean up any spelling or grammar mistakes that you might have made. Also, go ahead and erase any brainstorming ideas that you weren't able to expand upon and clean up any other extraneous information that you might have written that doesn't fit into your paper.

As you proofread, make sure there aren't any fragments or run-ons. Check for sentences that are too short or too long. If the sentence is too short, look to see if you have an identifiable subject and verb. If it is too long, break it up into two separate sentences. Watch out for any "big" words you may have used. It's good to use difficult vocabulary words, but only if you are positive that you are using them correctly. Your paper has to be correct, it doesn't have to be fancy. You're not trying to impress anyone with your vocabulary, just your ability to develop and express ideas.

Points of view

A point of view is the perspective the writer uses when writing. It is important to maintain the same point of view throughout an essay. Shifting points of view can confuse readers and cause the essay to be incoherent. A writer may choose one of three possible points of view. In the personal or first-person point of view, the writer uses the pronouns *I* or *we*. In the second-person point of view, the writer uses the pronoun *you*. In the third-person point of view, the idea is given more importance than the person who has the idea. For example, if using first person, a writer may write, *I believe that dogs are better pets than cats*. Using the second-person point of view, the writer would write, *If you have a dog, you know they make better pets than cats*. The same idea in third person would read, *Dogs make better pets than cats*.

Argumentative writing

Constructing a reasonable argument, the goal is not to "win" or have the last word, but rather to reveal current understanding of the question, and propose a solution to the perceived problem. The purpose of argument in a free society or a research field is to reach the best conclusion possible at the time.

Conventions of arguments vary from culture to culture. In America arguments tend to be direct rather than subtle, carefully organized rather than discursive, spoken plainly rather than poetically. Evidence presented is usually specific and factual, while appeals to intuition or communal wisdom are rare.

Argumentative writing takes a stand on a debatable issue , and seeks to explore all sides of the issue and reach the best possible solution. Argumentative writing should not be combative, at it's strongest it is assertive. A prelude to argumentative writing is an examination of the issue's social and intellectual contexts.

Introduction

The introduction of an essay arguing an issue should end with a thesis sentence that states a position on the issue. A good strategy is to establish credibility with readers by showing both expert knowledge and fair-mindedness. Building common ground with undecided or neutral readers is helpful.

The thesis should be supported by strong arguments that support the stated position. The main lines of argument should have a cumulative effect of convincing readers that the thesis has merit. The sum of the main lines of argument will outline the overall argumentative essay. The outline will clearly illustrate the central thesis, and subordinate claims that support it.

Evidence must be provided that support both the thesis and supporting arguments. Evidence based on reading should be documented, to show the sources. Readers must know how to check sources for accuracy and validity.

Supporting evidence

Most arguments must be supported by facts and statistics. Facts are something that is known with certainty, and have been objectively verified. Statistics may be used in selective ways to for partisan purposes. It is good to check statistics by reading authors writing on both sides of an issue. This will give a more accurate idea of how valid are the statistics cited.

Examples and illustrations add an emotional component to arguments, reaching readers in ways that facts and figures cannot. They are most effective when used in combination with objective information that can be verified.

Expert opinion can contribute to a position on a question. The source should be an authority whose credentials are beyond dispute. Sometimes it is necessary to provide the credentials of the expert. Expert testimony can be quoted directly, or may be summarized by the writer. Sources must be well documented to insure their validity.

Counter arguments

In addition to arguing a position, it is a good practice to review opposing arguments and attempt to counter them. This process can take place anywhere in the essay, but is perhaps best placed after the thesis is stated. Objections can be countered on a point-by-point analysis, or in a summary paragraph. Pointing out flaws in counter arguments is important, as is showing the counter arguments to have less weight than the supported thesis.

Building common ground with neutral or opposed readers can make a strong case. Sharing values with undecided readers can allow people to switch positions without giving up what they feel is important. People who may oppose a position need to feel they can change their minds without compromising their intelligence or their integrity. This appeal to open-mindedness can be a powerful tool in arguing a position without antagonizing opposing views.

Fallacious arguments

A number of unreasonable argumentative tactics are known as logical fallacies. Most fallacies are misguided uses of legitimate argumentative arguments.

Generalizing is drawing a conclusion from an array of facts using inductive reasoning. These conclusions are a probability, not a certainty. The fallacy known as a "hasty generalization" is a conclusion based on insufficient or unrepresentative evidence. Stereotyping is a hasty generalization about a group. This is common because of the human tendency to perceive selectively. Observations are made through a filter of preconceptions, prejudices, and attitudes.

Analogies point out similarities between disparate things. When an analogy is unreasonable, it is called a "false analogy". This usually consists of assuming if two things are alike in one respect, they must be alike in others. This, of course, may or may not be true. Each comparison must be independently verified to make the argument valid.

Post Hoc Fallacy

Tracing cause and effect can be a complicated matter. Because of the complexity involved, writers often over-simplify it. A common error is to assume that because one event follows another, the first is the cause of the second. This common fallacy is known as "post hoc", from the Latin meaning "after this, therefore because of this".

A post hoc fallacy could run like this: "Since Abner Jones returned to the Giants lineup, the team has much better morale". The fact that Jones returned to the lineup may or may not have had an effect on team morale. The writer must show there is a cause and effect relationship between Jones' return and team morale. It is not enough to note that one event followed another. It must be proved beyond a reasonable doubt that morale was improved by the return of Jones to the lineup. The two may be true but do not necessarily follow a cause and effect pattern.

Assumptions

When considering problems and solutions, the full range of possible options should be mentioned before recommending one solution above others. It is unfair to state there are only two alternatives, when in fact there are more options. Writers who set up a choice between their preferred option and a clearly inferior one are committing the "either...or" fallacy. All reasonable alternatives should be included in the possible solutions.

Assumptions are claims that are taken to be true without proof. If a claim is controversial, proof should be provided to verify the assumption. When a claim is made that few would agree with, the writer is guilty of a "non sequitur" (Latin for "does not follow") fallacy. Thus any assumption that is subject to debate cannot be accepted without supporting evidence is suspect.

Syllogism

Deductive reasoning is constructed in a three-step method called a syllogism. The three steps are the major premise, the minor premise, and the conclusion. The major premise is a generalization, and the minor premise is a specific case. The conclusion is deduced from applying the generalization to the specific case. Deductive arguments fail if either the major or minor premise is not true, or if the conclusion does not logically follow from the premises. This means a deductive argument must stand on valid, verifiable premises, and the conclusion is a logical result of the premises.

"Straw man" fallacy

The "straw man" fallacy consists of an oversimplification or distortion of opposing views. This fallacy is one of the most obvious and easily uncovered since it relies on gross distortions. The name comes from a side setting up a position so weak (the straw man) that is easily refuted.

Sentences

The largest structural unit normally recognized by grammar is the sentence. Any attempt to accurately define the sentence is in error. Any such definition will not bear up under Linguistic Analysis. In every language, there are a limited number of favorite sentence-types to which most others can be related. They vary from language to language. Certain utterances, while not immediately conforming to favorite sentence types, can be expanded in their context to become one sentence of a particular type. These can be called referable sentences. Other utterances that do not conform to favorite sentence types may reveal obsolete sentence types; these are proverbial sayings and are called gnomic or fossilized sentences. A very small number of utterances not conforming to the favorite sentence-types are found in prescribed social situations, such as "Hello" or "Bye".

Sentence patterns

Sentence patterns fall into five common modes with some exceptions. They are:

- Subject / linking verb / subject complement
- Subject / transitive verb / direct object
- Subject / transitive verb / indirect object / direct object

- Subject / transitive verb / direct object / object complement
- Subject / intransitive verb

Common exceptions to these patterns are questions and commands, sentences with delayed subjects, and passive transformations. Writers sometimes use the passive voice when the active voice would be more appropriate.

Sentences classification

Sentences are classified in two ways:

a. according to their structure
b. according to their purpose

Writers use declarative sentences to make statements, imperative sentences to issue requests or commands, interrogative sentences to ask questions, and exclamatory sentences to make exclamations.

Depending on the number and types of clauses they contain, sentences may be classified as simple, compound, complex, or compound-complex.

Clauses come in two varieties: independent and subordinate.

- An independent clause is a full sentence pattern that does not function within another sentence pattern; it contains a subject and modifiers plus a verb and any objects, complements, and modifiers of that verb. It either stands alone or could stand alone.
- A subordinate clause is a full sentence pattern that functions within a sentence as an adjective, an adverb, or a noun but that cannot stand alone as a complete sentence.

Sentence structures

The four major types of sentence structure are:

1. Simple sentences - Simple sentences have one independent clause with no subordinate clauses. a simple sentence may contain compound elements,- a compound subject, verb, or object for example, but does not contain more than one full sentence pattern.

2. Compound sentences - Compound sentences are composed of two or more independent clauses with no subordinate clauses. The independent clauses are usually joined with a comma and a coordinating conjunction, or with a semicolon.

3. Complex sentences - A complex sentence is composed of one independent clause with one or more dependent clauses.

4. Compound-complex sentences - A compound-complex sentence contains at least two independent clauses and at least one subordinate clause. sometimes they contain two full sentence patters that can stand alone. When each independent clause contains a subordinate clause, this makes the sentence both compound and complex.

Chomsky's sentence structure

Deep structure is a representation of the syntax of a sentence distinguished by various criteria from its surface structure. Initially defined by Noam Chomsky as the part of the syntactic description of a of a sentence that determines its semantic interpretation by the base component of a generative grammar.

Surface sentence structure is a representation of the syntax of a sentence seen as deriving by one ore more transformations, from a an underlying deep structure. Such a sentence is in the order in which the corresponding phonetic forms are spoken. Surface structure was later broadened by Chomsky to include semantic structure. Chomsky's later minimalist program no longer takes this for granted. Minimalist theory assumes no more than a minimum of types of statements and levels of representation.

The technical analysis outlined by Chomsky over three decades forms an integral part of transformational grammar.

Word confusion

"Which" should be used to refer to things only.

John's dog, which was called Max, is large and fierce.

"That" may be used to refer to either persons or things.

Is this the only book that Louis L'Amour wrote?

Is Louis L'Amour the author that [or who] wrote Western novels?

"Who" should be used to refer to persons only.

Mozart was the composer who [or that] wrote those operas.

Parts of speech

Nouns

Nouns are the name of a person, place, or thing, and are usually signaled by an article (a, an, the). Nouns sometimes function as adjectives modifying other nouns. Nouns used in this manner are called noun/adjectives. Nouns are classified for a number of purposes: capitalization, word choice, count/no count nouns, and collective nouns are examples.

Pronouns

Pronouns is a word used in place of a noun. Usually the pronoun substitutes for the specific noun, called the antecedent. Although most pronouns function as substitutes for nouns, some can function as adjectives modifying nouns. pronouns may be classed as personal, possessive, intensive, relative, interrogative, demonstrative, indefinite, and reciprocal. pronouns can cause a number of problems for writers including pronoun-antecedent agreement, distinguishing between who and whom, and differentiating pronouns such as I and me.

> ➤ **Review Video: <u>Nouns and Pronouns</u>**
> *Visit **mometrix.com/academy** and enter **Code: 312073***

Problems with pronouns

Pronouns are words that substitute for nouns: he, it, them, her, me, and so on. Four frequently encountered problems with pronouns include:

- Pronoun - antecedent agreement - The antecedent of a pronoun is the word the pronoun refers to. A pronoun and its antecedent agree when they are both singular or plural.

- Pronoun reference - A pronoun should refer clearly to its antecedent. A pronoun's reference will be unclear if it id ambiguous, implied, vague, or indefinite.

- Personal pronouns - Some pronouns change their case form according to their grammatical structure in a sentence. Pronouns functioning as subjects appear in the subjective case, those functioning as objects appear in the objective case, and those functioning as possessives appear in the possessive case.

- Who or whom - Who, a subjective-case pronoun, can only be used subjects and subject complements. Whom, an objective case pronoun, can only be used for objects. The words who and whom appear primarily in subordinate clauses or in questions.

Verbs

The verb of a sentence usually expresses action or being. It is composed of a main verb and sometimes supporting verbs. These helping verbs are forms of have, do, and be, and nine modals. The modals are "can, could, may, might, shall, should, will, would, and ought". Some verbs are followed by words that look like prepositions, but are so closely associated with the verb to be part of its meaning. These words are known as particles, and examples include "call off", "look up", and "drop off".

The main verb of a sentence is always one that would change form from base form to past tense, past participle, present participle and, -s forms. When both the past-tense and past-participle forms of a verb end in "ed", the verb is regular. In all other cases the verb is irregular. The verb "be" is highly irregular, having eight forms instead of the usual five.

- Linking verbs link the subject to a subject complement, a word or word group that completes the meaning of the subject by renaming or describing it.

- A transitive verb takes a direct object, a word or word group that names a receiver of the action. The direct object of a transitive verb is sometimes preceded by an indirect object. Transitive verbs usually appear in the active voice, with a subject doing the action and a direct object receiving the action. The direct object of a transitive verb is sometimes followed by an object complement, a word or word group that completes the direct object's meaning by renaming or describing it.

- Intransitive verbs take no objects or complements. Their pattern is subject verb.

A dictionary will disclose whether a verb is transitive or intransitive. Some verbs have both transitive and intransitive functions.

> **Review Video:** <u>Action Verbs and Linking Verbs</u>
> *Visit **mometrix.com/academy** and enter **Code: 743142***

<u>Verb phrases</u>

A verbal phrase is a verb form that does not function as the verb of a clause. There are three major types of verbal phrases:

- Participial phrases - These always function as adjectives. Their verbals are always present participles, always ending in "ing", or past participles frequently ending in "-d,-ed,-n.-en,or -t". Participial phrases frequently appear immediately following the noun or pronoun they modify.

- Gerund phrases - Gerund phrases are built around present participles and they always function as nouns. : usually as subjects subject complements, direct objects, or objects of a preposition.

- Infinitive phrases are usually structured around "to" plus the base form of the verb. they can function as nouns, as adjectives, or as adverbs. When functioning as a noun, an infinitive phrase may appear in almost any noun slot in a sentence, usually as a subject, subject complement, or direct object. Infinitive phrases functioning as adjectives usually appear immediately following the noun or pronoun they modify. adverbial phrases usually qualify the meaning of the verb.

Problems with verbs

The verb is the heart of the sentence. Verbs have several potential problems including:

- Irregular verbs - Verbs that do not follow usual grammatical rules.
- Tense - Tenses indicate the time of an action in relation to the time of speaking or writing about the action.
- Mood - There are three moods in English: the indicative, used for facts, opinions, and questions; the imperative, used for orders or advice, and the subjunctive, used for wishes. The subjective mood is the most likely to cause problems. The subjective mood is used for wishes, and in "if" clauses expressing conditions contrary to facts. The subjective in such cases is the past tense form of the verb; in the case of "be", it is always "were", even if the subject is singular. The subjective mood is also used in "that' clauses following verbs such as "ask, insist, recommend, and request. The subjunctive in such cases is the base or dictionary form of the verb.

Adjectives

An adjective is a word use to modify or describe a noun or pronoun. An adjective usually answers one of these question: "Which one?, What kind of?, and How many?" Adjectives usually precede the words they modify, although they sometimes follow linking verbs, in which case they describe the subject. Most adjectives have three forms: the positive, the comparative, and the superlative. The comparative should be used to compare two things, the superlative to compare three or more things.

> ➤ **Review Video: What is an Adjective?**
> *Visit **mometrix.com/academy** and enter **Code: 470154***

Articles

Articles, sometimes classed as nouns, are used to mark nouns. There are only three: the definite article "the," and the indefinite articles "a", and "and".

Adverbs

An adverb is a word used to modify or qualify a verb, adjective, or another adverb. It usually answers one of these questions: "When?, where?, how?, and why?" Adverbs modifying adjectives or other adverbs usually intensify or limit the intensity of words they modify. The negators "not" and "never" are classified as adverbs. Writers sometimes misuse adverbs, and multilingual speakers have trouble placing them correctly. Most adverbs also have three forms: the positive, the comparative, and the superlative. The comparative should be used to compare two things, the superlative to compare three or more things.

> **Review Video: <u>Adverbs</u>**
> *Visit **mometrix.com/academy** and enter **Code: 713951***

Prepositions

A preposition is a word placed before a noun or pronoun to form a phrase modifying another word in the sentence. The prepositional phrase usually functions as an adjective or adverb. There are a limited number of prepositions in English, perhaps around 80. Some prepositions are more than one word long. "Along with", "listen to", and "next to" are some examples.

> **Review Video: <u>What is a Preposition?</u>**
> *Visit **mometrix.com/academy** and enter **Code: 946763***

Conjunctions

Conjunctions join words, phrases, or clauses, and they indicate the relationship between the elements that are joined. There are coordinating conjunctions that connect grammatically equal element, correlative conjunctions that connect pairs, subordinating conjunctions that introduces a subordinate clause, and conjunctive adverbs which may be used with a semicolon to connect independent clauses. The most common conjunctive adverbs include "then, thus, and however". Using adverbs correctly helps avoid sentence fragments and run-on sentences.

Subjects

The subject of a sentence names who or what the sentence is about. The complete subject is composed of the simple subject and all of its modifiers.

To find the complete subject, ask "Who" or "What", and insert the verb to complete the question. The answer is the complete subject. To find the simple subject, strip away all the modifiers in the complete subject.

In imperative sentences, the verb's subject is understood but not actually present in the sentence. Although the subject ordinarily comes before the verb, sentences that begin with "There are" or "There was", the subject follows the verb.

The ability to recognize the subject of a sentence helps in editing a variety of problems such as sentence fragments and subject-verb agreement, as well as the choice of pronouns.

> **Review Video: Subjects**
> *Visit **mometrix.com/academy** and enter **Code:** **444771***

Subordinate word groups

Subordinate word groups cannot stand alone. They function only within sentences, as adjectives, adverbs, or nouns.

- Prepositional phrases begins with a preposition and ends with a noun or noun equivalent called its object. Prepositional phrases function as adjectives or adverbs.
- Subordinate clauses are patterned like sentences, having subject, verbs, and objects or complements. They function within sentences as adverbs, adjectives, or nouns.
- Adjective clauses modify nouns or pronouns and begin with a relative pronoun or relative adverb.
- Adverb clauses modify verbs, adjectives, and other adverbs.
- Noun clauses function as subjects, objects, or complements. In both adjective and noun clauses words may appear out of their normal order. The parts of a noun clause may also appear in their normal order.

Appositive and absolute phrases

Strictly speaking, appositive phrases are not subordinate word groups. Appositive phrases function somewhat as adjectives do, to describe nouns or pronouns. Instead of modifying nouns or pronouns however, appositive phrases rename them. In form they are nouns or nouns equivalents. Appositives are said to be in " in apposition" to the nouns or pronouns they rename. For example, in the sentence "Terriers, hunters at heart, have been dandled up to look like lap dogs", "hunters at heart" is apposition to the noun "terriers".

An absolute phrase modifies a whole clause or sentence, not just one word, and it may appear nearly anywhere in the sentence. It consists of a noun or noun equivalent usually followed by a participial phrase. Both appositive and absolute phrases can cause confusion in their usage in grammatical structures. They are particularly difficult for a person whose first language is not English.

Correct pronoun usage in combinations

To determine the correct pronoun form in a compound subject, try each subject separately with the verb, adapting the form as necessary. Your ear will tell you which form is correct. *Example*:

Bob and (I, me) will be going.

Restate the sentence twice, using each subject individually. Bob will be going. I will be going.

"Me will be going" does not make sense.

When a pronoun is used with a noun immediately following (as in "we boys"), say the sentence without the added noun. Your ear will tell you the correct pronoun form. *Example*:

(We/Us) boys played football last year.

Restate the sentence twice, without the noun. We played football last year. Us played football last year. Clearly "We played football last year" makes more sense.

Prefixes and Suffixes

Prefix	Meaning	Examples
A	in, on, of, up, to	abed, afoot
A	without, lacking	atheist, agnostic
Ab	from, away, off	abdicate, abjure
Ad	to, toward	advance
Am	friend, love	amicable, amatory
Ante	before, previous	antecedent, antedate
anti	against, opposing	antipathy, antidote
auto	self	autonomy, autobiography
belli	war, warlike	bellicose
bene	well, good	benefit, benefactor
bi	two	bisect, biennial
bio	life	biology, biosphere
cata	down, away, thoroughly	catastrophe, cataclysm
chron	time	chronometer, synchronize
circum	around	circumspect, circumference
com	with, together, very	commotion, complicate
contra	against, opposing	contradict, contravene
cred	belief, trust	credible, credit
de	from	depart
dem	people	demographics, democracy
dia	through, across, apart	diameter, diagnose
dis	away, off, down, not	dissent, disappear
epi	upon	epilogue
equi	equal, equally	equivalent
ex	out	extract
for	away, off, from	forget, forswear
fore	before, previous	foretell, forefathers
homo	same, equal	homogenized
hyper	excessive, over	hypercritical, hypertension
hypo	under, beneath	hypodermic, hypothesis
in	in, into	intrude, invade
in	not, opposing	incapable, ineligible
inter	among, between	intercede, interrupt
intra	within	intramural, intrastate
magn	large	magnitude, magnify
mal	bad, poorly, not	malfunction
micr	small	microbe, microscope
mis	bad, poorly, not	misspell, misfire
mono	one, single	monogomy, monologue
mor	die, death	mortality, mortuary
neo	new	neolithic, neoconservative
non	not	nonentity, nonsense
ob	against, opposing	objection
omni	all, everywhere	omniscient

Prefix	Meaning	Examples
ortho	right, straight	orthogonal, orthodox
over	above	overbearing
pan	all, entire	panorama, pandemonium
para	beside, beyond	parallel, paradox
per	through	perceive, permit
peri	around	periscope, perimeter
phil	love, like	philosophy, philanthropic
poly	many	polymorphous, polygamous
post	after, following	postpone, postscript
pre	before, previous	prevent, preclude
prim	first, early	primitive, primary
pro	forward, in place of	propel, pronoun
re	back, backward, again	revoke, recur
retro	back, backward	retrospect, retrograde
semi	half, partly	semicircle, semicolon
sub	under, beneath	subjugate, substitute
super	above, extra	supersede, supernumerary
sym	with, together	sympathy, symphony
trans	across, beyond, over	transact, transport
ultra	beyond, excessively	ultramodern, ultrasonic, ultraviolet
un	not, reverse of	unhappy, unlock
uni	one	uniform, unity
vis	to see	visage, visable

Suffix	Meaning	Examples
able	able to, likely	capable, tolerable
age	process, state, rank	passage, bondage
ance	act, condition, fact	acceptance, vigilance
arch	to rule	monarch
ard	one that does excessively	drunkard, wizard
ate	having, showing	separate, desolate
ation	action, state, result	occupation, starvation
cy	state, condition	accuracy, captaincy
dom	state, rank, condition	serfdom, wisdom
en	cause to be, become	deepen, strengthen
er	one who does	teacher
esce	become, grow, continue	convalesce, acquiesce
esque	in the style of, like	picturesque, grotesque
ess	feminine	waitress, lioness
fic	making, causing	terrific, beatific
ful	full of, marked by	thankful, zestful
fy	make, cause, cause to have	glorify, fortify
hood	state, condition	manhood, statehood
ible	able, likely, fit	edible, possible, divisible
ion	action, result, state	union, fusion
ish	suggesting, like	churlish, childish
ism	act, manner, doctrine	barbarism, socialism
ist	doer, believer	monopolist, socialist
ition	action, state, result	sedition, expedition
ity	state, quality, condition	acidity, civility
ize	make, cause to be, treat with	sterilize, mechanize, criticize
less	lacking, without	hopeless, countless
like	like, similar	childlike, dreamlike
logue	type of speaking or writing	prologue
ly	like, of the nature of	friendly, positively
ment	means, result, action	refreshment, disappointment
ness	quality, state	greatness, tallness
or	doer, office, action	juror, elevator, honor
ous	marked by, given to	religious, riotous
ship	the art or skill of	statesmanship
some	apt to, showing	tiresome, lonesome
th	act, state, quality	warmth, width
tude	quality, state, result	magnitude, fortitude
ty	quality, state	enmity, activity
ward	in the direction of	backward, homeward

Punctuation

If a section of text has an opening dash, parentheses, or comma at the beginning of a phrase, then you can be sure there should be a matching closing dash, parentheses, or comma at the end of the phrase. If items in a series all have commas between them, then any additional items in that series will also gain commas. Do not alternate punctuation. If a dash is at the beginning of a statement, then do not put a parenthesis at the ending of the statement.

Commas

Commas break the flow of text. To test whether they are necessary, while reading the text to yourself, pause for a moment at each comma. If the pauses seem natural, then the commas are correct. If they are not, then the commas are not correct.

> ➤ **Review Video: <u>Commas</u>**
> *Visit **mometrix.com/academy** and enter **Code: 644254***

<u>Nonessential clauses and phrases</u>

A comma should be used to set off nonessential clauses and nonessential participial phrases from the rest of the sentence. To determine if a clause is essential, remove it from the sentence. If the removal of the clause would alter the meaning of the sentence, then it is essential. Otherwise, it is nonessential.

Example:

   John Smith, who was a disciple of Andrew Collins, was a noted archeologist.

In the example above, the sentence describes John Smith's fame in archeology. The fact that he was a disciple of Andrew Collins is not necessary to that meaning. Therefore, separating it from the rest of the sentence with commas, is correct.

Do not use a comma if the clause or phrase is essential to the meaning of the sentence.

Example:

   Anyone who appreciates obscure French poetry will enjoy reading the book.

If the phrase "who appreciates obscure French poetry" is removed, the sentence would indicate that anyone would enjoy reading the book, not just those with an appreciation for obscure French poetry. However, the sentence implies that the book's enjoyment may not be for everyone, so the phrase is essential.

Another perhaps easier way to determine if the clause is essential is to see if it has a comma at its beginning or end. Consistent, parallel punctuation must be used, and so if you can determine a comma exists at one side of the clause, then you can be certain that a comma should exist on the opposite side.

Independent clauses

Use a comma before the words and, but, or, nor, for, yet when they join independent clauses. To determine if two clauses are independent, remove the word that joins them. If the two clauses are capable of being their own sentence by themselves, then they are independent and need a comma between them.
Example:

He ran down the street, and then he ran over the bridge.

He ran down the street. Then he ran over the bridge. These are both clauses capable of being their own sentence. Therefore a comma must be used along with the word "and" to join the two clauses together.

If one or more of the clauses would be a fragment if left alone, then it must be joined to another clause and does not need a comma between them.
Example:

He ran down the street and over the bridge.

He ran down the street. Over the bridge. "Over the bridge" is a sentence fragment and is not capable of existing on its own. No comma is necessary to join it with "He ran down the street".

Note that this does not cover the use of "and" when separating items in a series, such as "red, white, and blue". In these cases a comma is not always necessary between the last two items in the series, but in general it is best to use one.

Parenthetical expressions

Commas should separate parenthetical expressions such as the following: after all, by the way, for example, in fact, on the other hand.

Example:

By the way, she is in my biology class.

If the parenthetical expression is in the middle of the sentence, a comma would be both before and after it.

Example:

She is, after all, in my biology class.

However, these expressions are not always used parenthetically. In these cases, commas are not used. To determine if an expression is parenthetical, see if it would need a pause if you were reading the text. If it does, then it is parenthetical and needs commas.

Example:

You can tell by the way she plays the violin that she enjoys its music.

No pause is necessary in reading that example sentence. Therefore the phrase "by the way" does not need commas around it.

Hyphens

Hyphenate a compound adjective that is directly before the noun it describes.

Example 1: He was the best-known kid in the school.

Example 2: The shot came from that grass-covered hill.

Example 3: The well-drained fields were dry soon after the rain.

Semicolons

<u>Period replacement</u>

A semicolon is often described as either a weak period or strong comma. Semicolons should separate independent clauses that could stand alone as separate sentences. To test where a semicolon should go, replace it with a period in your mind. If the two independent clauses would seem normal with the period, then the semicolon is in the right place.

Example:

The rain had finally stopped; a few rays of sunshine were pushing their way through the clouds.

The rain had finally stopped. A few rays of sunshine were pushing their way through the clouds. These two sentences can exist independently with a period between them. Because they are also closely related in thought, a semicolon is a good choice to combine them.

<u>Transitions</u>

When a semicolon is next to a transition word, such as "however", it comes before the word.

Example:

The man in the red shirt stood next to her; however, he did not know her name.

If these two clauses were separated with a period, the period would go before the word "however" creating the following two sentences: The man in the red shirt stood next to her. However, he did not know her name. The semicolon can function as a weak period and join the two clauses by replacing the period.

Some questions include a sentence with part or all of it underlined. Your answer choices will offer different ways to reword or rephrase the underlined portion of the sentence.

These questions will test your ability of correct and effective expression. Choose your answer carefully, utilizing the standards of written English, including grammar rules, the proper choice of words and of sentence construction. The correct answer will flow smoothly and be both clear and concise.

Modern Language Association style

The Modern Language Association style is widely used in literature and languages as well as other fields. The MLA style calls for noting brief references to sources in parentheses in the text of an essay, and adding an alphabetical list of sources, called "Works Cited", at the end. Specific recommendations of the MLA include:

- Works Cited - Includes only works actually cited. List on a separate page with the author's name, title, and publication information, which must list the location of the publisher, the publishers' name, and the date of publication.
- Parenthetical Citations - MLA style uses parenthetical citations following each quotation, reference, paraphrase, or summary to a source. Each citation is made up of the author's last name and page reference, keyed to a reference in "Works Cited".
- Explanatory Notes - Explanatory notes are numbered consecutively, and identified by superscript numbers in the text. The full notes may appear as endnotes or as footnotes at the bottom of the page.

American Psychological Association style

The American Psychological Association style is widely followed in the social sciences. The APA parenthetical citations within the text directs readers to a list of sources. In APA style this list is called "References". References are listed on a separate page, and each line includes the author's name, publication date, title, and publication information. Publication information includes the city where the publisher is located, and the publisher's name. Underline the titles of books and periodicals , but not articles.

APA parenthetical expressions citations include the author's last name, the date of publication, and the page number. APA style allows for content footnotes for information needed to be expanded or supplemented, marked in the text by superscript numbers in consecutive order. Footnotes are listed under a separate page, headed "Footnotes" after the last page of text. All entries should be double-spaced.

Final note

Depending on your test taking preferences and personality, the essay writing will probably be your hardest or your easiest section. You are required to go through the entire process of writing a paper very quickly, which can be quite a challenge.

Focus upon each of the steps listed above. Go through the process of creative flow first, generating ideas and thoughts about the topic. Then organize those ideas into a smooth logical flow. Pick out the ones that are best from the list you have created. Decide which main idea or angle of the topic you will discuss.

Create a recognizable structure in your paper, with an introductory paragraph explaining what you have decided upon, and what your main points will be. Use the body paragraphs to expand on those main points and have a conclusion that wraps up the issue or topic.

Save a few moments to go back and review what you have written. Clean up any minor mistakes that you might have had and give it those last few critical touches that can make a huge difference. Finally, be proud and confident of what you have written!

Practice Test Questions

Mathematics

1. If $y = 2$, what is the value of the following expression?

   $(y^9 / y^3) \times 2$

   A. 128
   B. 16
   C. 8192
   D. 1008

2. Simplify the following:

   $$\frac{16x^3 - 32x^2 + 8x}{4x}$$

   A. $4x^3 - 8x^2 + 2x$
   B. $12x^2 - 28x^2 + 4$
   C. $4x^2 - 8x + 2$
   D. $4x^2 + 8x + 2$

3. $x^2 + 8x + 16 = 0$

   Solve for x.

   A. $x = -4, 4$
   B. $x = 4$
   C. $x = -4$
   D. $x = -2, 2$

4. Use factoring to simplify the following:

   $x^2 + 7x + 12$

   A. $(x + 6)(x + 2)$
   B. $(x + 4)(x + 3)$
   C. $(x + 6)(x + 1)$
   D. $(x + 5)(x + 2)$

5. If $a = -6$ and $b = 7$, then $4a(3b+5)+2b=?$

   A. 638
   B. -485
   C. 850
   D. -610

6. Given a line with slope $m = -2$ that passes through the point (-3, 4), find the equation of the line in standard form.

   A. $2x + y - 2 = 0$
   B. $2x - y - 2 = 0$
   C. $2x + y + 2 = 0$
   D. $y = 2x + 2$

7. A line passes through points A (-3, 18) and B (5, 2). What is the slope of the line?
    A. 2
    B. -2
    C. 1/2
    D. -1/2

8. Which of the following numerals is not a prime number?
    A. 3
    B. 6
    C. 17
    D. 41

9. Which of the following is equal to the difference between 4^3 and 3^4?
    A. 0
    B. 1
    C. 27
    D. 17

10. What is the midpoint of points A (-20, 8) and B (5, 3)?
    A. (5.5, 7.5)
    B. (7.5, 5.5)
    C. (5.5, -7.5)
    D. (-7.5, 5.5)

11. Evaluate the following expression, if $x = 3$.
    $x^5x^2 + y^0 =$
    A. 59,049
    B. 59,050
    C. 2,187
    D. 2,188

12. $9x - 3y + 8xy - 3$
If $x = 10$ and $y = -2$, what is the value of this expression?
    A. -67
    B. -61
    C. -79
    D. 241

13. Simplify the following: $9x (3x^2 + 2x - 9)$
    A. $27x^2 + 18x - 81$
    B. $27x^3 + 18x^2 - 81x$
    C. $12x^3 + 11x^2 - x$
    D. $27x^3 + 18x^2 - 18x$

14. Expand the following expression: $(2x - 5) (x + 7)$
    A. $2x^2 + 9x - 35$
    B. $11x - 35$
    C. $2x^2 - 19x - 35$
    D. $2x^2 + 9x + 35$

15. What is the value of $2x^2 + 5x - y^2$ when $x = 3$ and $y = 5$?
    A. -4
    B. 8
    C. 16
    D. 72

16. $(y^2 + 9y - 2) + (4y^2 - y - 5) =$
    A. $5y^2 + 8y - 7$
    B. $5y^2 + 8y + 10$
    C. $5y^2 + 10y - 7$
    D. $5y^2 + 10y + 10$

17. If $x^2 + 5x = 6$, then $x = ?$
    A. -6 or -1
    B. -6 or 1
    C. -1 or 6
    D. 1 or 6

18. What percent of 56 is 42?
    A. 60%
    B. 72.5%
    C. 75%
    D. 85%

19. What is 56% of 25?
    A. 10
    B. 11
    C. 12
    D. 14

20. Solve the following equation, $5(80 / 8) + (7 - 2) - (9 \times 5) =$
    A. -150
    B. 10
    C. 100
    D. 230

21. Solve the following equation, $\dfrac{4 - (-12)}{-9 + 5} =$
    A. -8
    B. -4
    C. -2
    D. 4

22. If $x = 2y - 3$ and $2x + \dfrac{1}{2}y = 3$, then $y = ?$
    A. $-\dfrac{2}{3}$
    B. 1
    C. 2
    D. $\dfrac{18}{7}$

23. Solve for y using the following system of equations.
$2x - 6y = 12$
$-6x + 14y = 42$
A. -19.5
B. -52.5
C. -2.44
D. 6.56

24. If $6x + 2x - 26 = -5x$, then $\left[\frac{2x-1}{7}\right]^3 =$
A. 0.08
B. 0.19
C. 1.29
D. 12.7

25. If, $3(x + 14) = 4(x + 9)$, what does x equal?
A. $x = 4$
B. $x = 6$
C. $x = 12$
D. $x = 15$

26. Let $= \frac{x^4-2}{x^2+1}$. If x = -2, what is the value of y?
A. $-3\frac{3}{5}$
B. $2\frac{4}{5}$
C. $-2\frac{4}{5}$
D. $2\frac{2}{3}$

27. Which of the following expressions is a factor of the polynomial $x^2 - 4x - 21$?
A. $(x - 4)$
B. $(x - 3)$
C. $(x + 7)$
D. $(x - 7)$

28. What is the value of the y-intercept of the line described by the equation:
$2x + 3y - 7 = 0$?
A. 7
B. -7
C. $\frac{7}{3}$
D. $-\frac{7}{3}$

29. Which of the following is an expression equivalent to $\dfrac{a^8 b^{-9} c^2}{a^{-3} b^6 c^4}$?

   A. $\dfrac{a^5 c^2}{b^3}$

   B. $\dfrac{a^5}{b^3 c^2}$

   C. $\dfrac{a^5}{b^{15} c^2}$

   D. $\dfrac{a^{11}}{b^{15} c^2}$

30. Which of the following expressions is equivalent to $\sqrt[3]{8 x^5 y^7}$?

   A. $8^3 x^{15} y^{21}$

   B. $8^3 x^{\frac{5}{3}} y^{\frac{21}{3}}$

   C. $2 x^{15} y^{21}$

   D. $2 x^{\frac{5}{3}} y^{\frac{7}{3}}$

Reading

Read each passage carefully. Since the assessment is not timed, take as much time as you need to read each passage. Each passage may have one or more questions.

A helpful strategy is to focus on the opening and ending sentences of each paragraph to identify the main idea. Another strategy is to look for key words or phrases within the passage that indicate the author's purpose or the meaning.

Reading Sample Questions:

Read the selection and answer the questions that follow.

Cultivation of Tomato Plants

Tomato plants should be started in window boxes or greenhouses in late March so that they will be ready for the garden after the last frost. Use a soil of equal parts of sand, peat moss and manure, and plant the seeds about a quarter of an inch deep. After covering, water them through a cloth to protect the soil and cover the box with a pane of glass. Keep the box in a warm place for a few days, then place it in a sunny window. After the second leaf makes its appearance on the seedling, transplant the plant to another box, placing the seedlings two inches apart. Another alternative is to put the sprouted seedlings in four-inch pots, setting them deeper in the soil than they stood in the seed bed. To make the stem stronger, pinch out the top bud when the seedlings are four or five inches in height.

Finally, place the plants in their permanent positions after they have grown to be twelve or fifteen inches high. When transplanting, parts of some of the longest leaves should be removed. Large plants may be set five or six inches deep.

The soil should be fertilized the previous season. Fresh, stable manure, used as fertilizer, would delay the time of fruiting. To improve the condition of the soil, work in a spade full of old manure to a depth of at least a foot. Nitrate of soda, applied at about two hundred pounds per acre, may be used to give the plant a good start.

Plants grown on supports may be set two feet apart in the row, with the rows three or four feet apart depending upon the variety. Plants not supported by stakes or other methods should be set four feet apart.

Unsupported vines give a lighter yield and much of the fruit is likely to rot during the wet seasons. Use well sharpened stakes about two inches in diameter and five feet long. Drive the stakes into the ground at least six inches from the plants so that the roots will not be injured. Tie the tomato vines to the stakes with strings made out of strips of cloth, as twine is likely to cut them. Care must be taken not to wrap the limbs so tightly as to interfere with their growth. The training should start before the plants begin to trail on the ground.

1. What is the overall purpose of this passage?
    A. To describe how soil should be treated in order to plant tomatoes.
    B. To give an overview of how tomato plants are cultured.
    C. To teach the reader how to operate a farm.
    D. To describe a method of supporting tomato vines.

2. What does the passage imply as the reason that the seeds not planted outdoors immediately?
    A. A late freeze might kill the seedlings.
    B. The soil outdoors is too heavy for new seedlings.
    C. A heavy rain might wash away the seedlings.
    D. New seedlings need to be close to one another and then be moved apart later.

3. What would happen if the bud weren't pinched out of the seedlings when they are in individual pots?
    A. The plants would be weaker.
    B. The plants would freeze.
    C. The plants would need more water.
    D. The plants would not survive as long.

4. Why is old manure preferred to fresh manure?
    A. Fresh manure delays the plant's production of tomatoes.
    B. Fresh manure smells worse.
    C. Old manure is less expensive.
    D. Old manure mixes more readily with nitrate of soda.

5. What is the purpose of the last paragraph?
    A. To explain why unsupported plants give rotten fruit.
    B. To explain why cloth is used rather than wire.
    C. To describe in detail how tomato plants are cultured.
    D. To instruct the reader in the method of supporting tomato vines for culture.

Read the selection and answer the questions that follow.

Garth

The next morning she realized that she had slept. This surprised her – so long had sleep been denied her! She opened her eyes and saw the sun at the window. And then, beside it in the window, the deformed visage of Garth. Quickly, she shut her eyes again, feigning sleep. But he was not fooled. Presently she heard his voice, soft and kind: "Don't be afraid. I'm your friend. I came to watch you sleep, is all. There now, I am behind the wall. You can open your eyes."

The voice seemed pained and plaintive. The Hungarian opened her eyes, saw the window empty. Steeling herself, she arose, went to it, and looked out. She saw the man below, cowering by the wall, looking grief-stricken and

- 93 -

resigned. Making an effort to overcome her revulsion, she spoke to him as kindly as she could.

"Come," she said, but Garth, seeing her lips move, thought she was sending him away. He rose and began to lumber off, his eyes lowered and filled with despair.

"Come!" she cried again, but he continued to move off. Then, she swept from the cell, ran to him and took his arm. Feeling her touch, Garth trembled uncontrollably. Feeling that she drew him toward her, he lifted his supplicating eye and his whole face lit up with joy.

She drew him into the garden, where she sat upon a wall, and for a while they sat and contemplated one another. The more the Hungarian looked at Garth, the more deformities she discovered. The twisted spine, the lone eye, the huge torso over the tiny legs. She couldn't comprehend how a creature so awkwardly constructed could exist. And yet, from the air of sadness and gentleness that pervaded his figure, she began to reconcile herself to it.
"Did you call me back?" asked he.
"Yes," she replied, nodding. He recognized the gesture.
"Ah," he exclaimed. "Do you know that I am deaf?"
"Poor fellow," exclaimed the Hungarian, with an expression of pity.
"You'd think nothing more could be wrong with me," Garth put in, somewhat bitterly. But he was happier than he could remember having been.

6. During this passage, how do the girl's emotions toward Garth change?
    A. They go from anger to fear.
    B. They go from hatred to disdain.
    C. They go from fear to disdain.
    D. They go from revulsion to pity.

7. What is a synonym for the word *supplicating*?
    A. Castigating
    B. Menacing
    C. Repeating
    D. Begging

8. Which of the following adjectives would you use to describe Garth's feelings toward himself?
    A. Contemplative
    B. Destitute
    C. Unhappy
    D. Deflated

9. What two characteristics are contrasted in Garth?
    A. Ugliness and gentleness
    B. Fear and merriment
    C. Distress and madness
    D. Happiness and sadness

10. Why was the girl surprised that she had slept?
  A. She seldom slept.
  B. It had been a long time since she had had the chance to sleep.
  C. She hadn't intended to go to sleep.
  D. Garth looked so frightening that she thought he would keep her awake.

Read the selection and answer the questions that follow.

Leaving

Even though Martin and Beth's steps were muffled by the falling snow, Beth could still hear the faint crunch of leaves underneath. The hushed woods had often made Beth feel safe and at peace, but these days they just made her feel lonely.

"I'm glad we decided to hike the trail, Martin. It's so quiet and pretty."

"Sure."

Beth couldn't understand how it happened, but over the past few months this silence had grown between them, weighing down their relationship. Of course, there was that thing with Mary, but Beth had forgiven Martin. They moved on. It was in the past.

"Do you want to see a movie tonight?" asked Beth. "There's a new one showing at the downtown theater."

"Whatever you want."

She wanted her husband back. She wanted the laughter and games. She wanted the late-night talks over coffee. She wanted to forget Mary and Martin together. She wanted to feel some sort of <u>rapport</u> again.

"Is everything alright, Martin?"

"I'm fine. Just tired."

"We didn't have to come; we could have stayed at home."

"It's fine."

Beth closed her eyes, tilted her head back, and breathed in the crisp air. "Fine" once meant "very good," or "precious." Now, it is a meaningless word, an excuse not to tell other people what's on your mind. "Fine" had hung in the air between them for months now, a softly falling word that hid them from each other. Beth wasn't even sure she knew Martin anymore, but she was confident that it was only a matter of time before everything was not "fine," only a matter of time before he told her…

"I have to leave."

"Huh? What?"

"I got a page. My patient is going into cardiac arrest."

"I wish you didn't have to leave."

"I'm sorry, but I have to go."

"I know."

11. It is reasonable to infer that Martin and Beth's relationship is strained because:
  A. Martin recently lost his job.
  B. Martin was unfaithful to Beth.
  C. Martin works too much.
  D. Martin does not want to go to the movies.

12. According to Beth, the word "fine" means:
    A. "good"
    B. "precious"
    C. "very good"
    D. Nothing—it is a meaningless word.

13. The best definition of the underlined word *rapport* is:
    A. a close relationship.
    B. a sense of well-being.
    C. a common goal.
    D. loneliness.

14. Based on the passage, it is reasonable to infer that Martin is a:
    A. mechanic.
    B. medical doctor.
    C. dentist.
    D. film director.

15. Based on Beth's perception of her and Martin's relationship, it is reasonable to infer:
    A. Martin is dissatisfied with his job.
    B. Beth wants to have a baby.
    C. Martin is going to leave Beth.
    D. Martin and Beth have not known each other long.

Read the selection and answer the questions that follow.

New Zealand Inhabitants

The islands of New Zealand are among the most remote of all the Pacific islands. New Zealand is an archipelago, with two large islands and a number of smaller ones. Its climate is far cooler than the rest of Polynesia. Nevertheless, according to Maori legends, it was colonized in the early fifteenth century by a wave of Polynesian voyagers who traveled southward in their canoes and settled on North Island. At this time, New Zealand was already known to the Polynesians, who had probably first landed there some 400 years earlier.

The Polynesian southward migration was limited by the availability of food. Traditional Polynesian tropical crops such as taro and yams will grow on North Island, but the climate of South Island is too cold for them. Coconuts will not grow on either island. The first settlers were forced to rely on hunting and gathering, and, of course, fishing. Especially on South Island, most settlements remained close to the sea. At the time of the Polynesian influx, enormous flocks of moa birds had their rookeries on the island shores. These flightless birds were easy prey for the settlers, and within a few centuries had been hunted to extinction. Fish, shellfish and the roots of the fern were other important sources of food, but even these began to diminish in quantity as the human population increased. The Maori had few

- 96 -

other sources of meat: dogs, smaller birds, and rats. Archaeological evidence shows that human flesh was also eaten, and that tribal warfare increased markedly after the moa disappeared.

By far the most important farmed crop in prehistoric New Zealand was the sweet potato. This tuber is hearty enough to grow throughout the islands, and could be stored to provide food during the winter months, when other food-gathering activities were difficult. The availability of the sweet potato made possible a significant increase in the human population. Maori tribes often lived in encampments called *pa*, which were fortified with earthen embankments and usually located near the best sweet potato farmlands.

16. A definition for the word *archipelago* is
    A. A country
    B. A place in the southern hemisphere
    C. A group of islands
    D. A roosting place for birds

17. This article is primarily about what?
    A. The geology of New Zealand
    B. New Zealand's early history
    C. New Zealand's prehistory
    D. Food sources used by New Zealand's first colonists.

18. According to the passage, when was New Zealand first settled?
    A. In the fifteenth century
    B. Around the eleventh century
    C. Thousands of years ago
    D. By flightless birds

19. What was a significant difference between the sweet potato and other crops known to the Polynesians?
    A. The sweet potato provided more protein.
    B. The sweet potato would grow on North Island.
    C. The sweet potato could be stored during the winter.
    D. The sweet potato could be cultured near their encampments.

20. Why was it important that sweet potatoes could be stored?
    A. They could be eaten in winter, when other foods were scarce.
    B. They could be traded for fish and other goods.
    C. They could be taken along by groups of warriors going to war.
    D. They tasted better after a few weeks of storage.

21. What was it about the moa that made them easy for the Maori to catch?
    A. They were fat.
    B. They roosted by the shore.
    C. They were not very smart.
    D. They were unable to fly.

22. Why did early settlements remain close to the sea?
    A. The people liked to swim.
    B. The people didn't want to get far from the boats they had come in.
    C. Taro and yams grow only close to the beaches.
    D. They were dependent upon sea creatures for their food.

Read the selection and answer the questions that follow.

Daylight Saving Time

Daylight Saving Time (DST) is the practice of changing clocks so that afternoons have more daylight and mornings have less. Clocks are adjusted forward one hour in the spring and one hour backward in the fall. The main purpose of the change is to make better use of daylight.

DST began with the goal of conservation. Benjamin Franklin suggested it as a method of saving on candles. It was used during both World Wars to save energy for military needs. Although DST's potential to save energy was a primary reason behind its implementation, research into its effects on energy conservation are contradictory and unclear.

Beneficiaries of DST include all activities that can benefit from more sunlight after working hours, such as shopping and sports. A 1984 issue of Fortune magazine estimated that a seven-week extension of DST would yield an additional $30 million for 7-Eleven stores. Public safety may be increased by the use of DST: some research suggests that traffic fatalities may be reduced when there is additional afternoon sunlight.

On the other hand, DST complicates timekeeping and some computer systems. Tools with built-in time-keeping functions such as medical devices can be affected negatively. Agricultural and evening entertainment interests have historically opposed DST.

DST can affect health, both positively and negatively. It provides more afternoon sunlight in which to get exercise. It also impacts sunlight exposure; this is good for getting vitamin D, but bad in that it can increase skin cancer risk. DST may also disrupt sleep.

Today, daylight saving time has been adopted by more than one billion people in about 70 countries. DST is generally not observed in countries near the equator because sunrise times do not vary much there. Asia and Africa do not generally observe it. Some countries, such as Brazil, observe it only in some regions.

DST can lead to peculiar situations. One of these occurred in November, 2007 when a woman in North Carolina gave birth to one twin at 1:32 a.m. and, 34 minutes later, to the second twin. Because of DST and the time change at 2:00 a.m., the second twin was officially born at 1:06, 26 minutes earlier than her brother.

23. According to the passage, what is the main purpose of DST?
    A. To increase public safety
    B. To benefit retail businesses
    C. To make better use of daylight
    D. To promote good health

24. Which of the following is not mentioned in the passage as a negative effect of DST?
    A. Energy conservation
    B. Complications with time keeping
    C. Complications with computer systems
    D. Increased skin cancer risk

25. The article states that DST involves:
    A. Adjusting clocks forward one hour in the spring and the fall.
    B. Adjusting clocks backward one hour in the spring and the fall.
    C. Adjusting clocks forward in the fall and backward in the spring.
    D. Adjusting clocks forward in the spring and backward in the fall.

26. Which interests have historically opposed DST, according to the passage?
    A. retail businesses and sports
    B. evening entertainment and agriculture
    C. 7-Eleven and health
    D. medical devices and computing

27. According to the article, increased sunlight exposure:
    A. is only good for health.
    B. is only bad for health.
    C. has no effect on health.
    D. can be both good and bad for health.

28. What is an example given in the passage of a peculiar situation that DST has caused?
    A. sleep disruption
    B. driving confusion
    C. twin birth order complications
    D. countries with DST only in certain regions

29. For what purpose did Benjamin Franklin first suggest DST?
    A. to save money for military needs
    B. to save candles
    C. to reduce traffic fatalities
    D. to promote reading

30. In what region does the article state DST is observed only in some regions?
    A. The equator
    B. Asia
    C. Africa
    D. Brazil

Writing

Read the selection and answer the questions 1-5.

(1) I had the same teacher for both third and 4th grades, which were difficult years for me. (2) My teacher and I did not get along, and I don't think she liked me. (3) Every day, I thought she was treating me unfairly and being mean. (4) Because I felt that way, I think I acted out and stopped doing my work. (5) In the middle of fourth grade, my family moved to a new town, and I had Mr. Shanbourne as my new teacher.

(6) From the very first day in Mr. Shanbourne's class, I was on guard. (7) I was expecting to hate my teacher and for him to hate me back when I started his class. (8) Mr. Shanbourne took me by surprise right away when he asked me if I wanted to stand up and introduce myself. (9) I said no, probably in a surly voice, and he just nodded and began teaching the first lesson of the day.

(10) I wasn't sure how to take this. (11) My old teacher forced me to do things and gave me detention if I didn't. (12) She loved detention and gave it to me for anything I did--talking back, working too loudly, forgetting an assignment. (13) Mr. Shanbourne obviously didn't believe in detention, and I tried him! (14) During my first two weeks at my new school I did my best to get in trouble. (15) I zoned out in class, turned work in late, talked out in class, and handed in assignments after the due date. (16) Every time, Mr. Shanbourne just nodded.

(17) Mr. Shanbourne asked me to stay in during recess. (18) *This is it*, I thought. I was going to get in trouble, get the detention my ten-year-old self had practically been begging for. (19) After all of the other kids ran outside, I walked up to Mr. Shanbourne's desk.

(20) "How are you doing, Alberto," he said.

(21) I mumbled something.

(22) He told me he was disappointed in my behavior over the last two weeks. (23) I had expected this and just took it. (24) The detention was coming any second. (25) Than Mr. Shanbourne took me by surprise. (26) He told me that even though he didn't know me very well, he believed I could be a hard worker and that I could be successful in his class. (27) He asked me how he could help listen better and turn my work in on time.

(28) I told him I had to think about it and rushed out to recess. (29) Even though my answer seemed rude, I was stunned. (30) I hadn't had a teacher in years who seemed to care about me, and said he believed in my abilities.

(31) To be honest, my behavior did not improve right away and I still turned in many of my assignments late. (32) But over the last few months of fourth

grade, things changed. (33) Mr. Shanbourne continued to believe in me and encuorage me and help me, and I responded by doing my best. (34) I had a different teacher for fifth grade, but whenever I was struggling I walked down to Mr. Shanbourne's classroom to get his advice. (35) I'll never forget how Mr. Shanbourne helped me, and I hope he'll never forget me either.

1. What change should be made to sentence 1?
   A. Change *teacher* to *teachers*
   B. Change *4th* to *fourth*
   C. Delete the comma after *grades*
   D. Change *years* to *year's*

2. What is the most effective way to revise sentence 7?
   A. I started his class expecting my teacher to hate me back and for me to hate him.
   B. Expecting to hate my teacher, I started his class expecting him to hate me back.
   C. Starting his class expecting to hate my teacher, I also expected to hate him back.
   D. I started his class expecting to hate my teacher and for him to hate me back.

3. What is the most effective way to combine sentences 10 and 11?
   A. I wasn't sure how to take this, and my old teacher forced me to do things and gave me detention if I didn't.
   B. I wasn't sure how to take this, although my old teacher forced me to do things and gave me detention if I didn't.
   C. I wasn't sure how to take this because my old teacher forced me to do things and gave me detention if I didn't.
   D. I wasn't sure how to take this as a result of my old teacher forced me to do things and gave me detention if I didn't.

4. Which phrase, if any, can be deleted from sentence 15 without changing the meaning of the sentence?
   A. zoned out in class
   B. talked out in class
   C. handed in assignments after the due date
   D. No change

5. What transition should be added to the beginning of sentence 16?
   A. However
   B. Actually
   C. Furthermore
   D. Eventually

6. Which of the following choices best completes the sentence?

When at last Amber was able to _____ the numerous difficulties associated with the task, she concluded the wisdom of her grandfather was not only desirable, but absolutely necessary.

   A. perceive
   B. perception
   C. perceptive
   D. perceived

7. Which of the following words best completes the sentence?

The plan seemed flawless until its execution. The flames from the modified grill licked the bottom portion of the new wooden deck. Emil's elation warped into horror as he began to sweat. His grandparents had been extremely angry with the experiment on their car and his grandfather's red face hung before his eyes like a dark vision: "Before you _____ some other wild plan, talk to me first so we don't need to bring in the fire department."

    A. concoct
    B. invent
    C. make
    D. design

8. Which of the following sentences shows the correct usage of the hyphen?
    A. Miriam was a real-estate-broker with Hendry and Henderson, so she understood the importance of a well-cared-for home.
    B. Felipe dialed Joyce's number since it was easy-to-remember and listened with baited breath.
    C. Although Biraju was not an accident-prone person, he knew his older brother did not share this trait.
    D. James and Henry, both twenty-one year old students, had been able to pass the difficult test for medical school.

9. Which of the following choices is misspelled?
    A. conciliatory
    B. paroxism
    C. malevolence
    D. pernicious

10. Which of the following word choices completes the sentence?

Matthew posted the notice in the main hall and then proceeded to pass out the rest of the invitations to the _____ until his backpack was empty.

    A. receive
    B. reception
    C. receivable
    D. receiving

11. Read the following topic sentence from an opinion piece. Which of the following choices could provide some support for the topic sentence?

"Expansionary monetary policies are not the best option during a recession."

    A. Increasing the money supply may serve temporarily to boost the economy, but such an action damages the value of the dollar in the long run.
    B. Basing fiscal decisions on government tax cuts is similar to deciding suddenly that one does not require additional income, and therefore no longer accepting dividend payments.
    C. Allowing the government to control an entire industry would fly in the face of the Founding Fathers, since it not only takes away liberties but also puts businesses in the hands of politicians.
    D. Decreasing the interest rates may be the only successful way to drive business to the banks, and encouraging small business long has been known to generate wealth.

12. Read the claim below. Which of the following supports a counterclaim?

"Schools need to provide year-round education for students. Since the evolution of our society has moved us from an agrarian population to a largely urban one, there is no longer any need for the two month break during the summer. It is, in fact, a waste of students'—and society's— precious time."

    A. The prospect of a year-round education for students is akin to an endless prison sentence; however, the inmates in this case cannot speak for themselves. They are the most vulnerable among us, and there is no one who will be their voice in this debate. Let's face it. This debate isn't about longer school days to help children, it's about providing more funding to the school staff.
    B. There's a reason teachers are fleeing the public school system. It's broken. Teachers often work long hours in difficult conditions—imagine having the occupant of your office throw a paper airplane at you while you are working—and get paid little. A longer school day punishes teachers who are already sweating blood over their occupation. Teachers not only work through the school day, but often spend hours at home, developing curricula, grading papers, and preparing for the following day.
    C. The limitations of this view are clear: there are no scientifically-backed works establishing that students perform better if they spend more time in school. However, there is significant research establishing the idea that learners do require time for creative pursuits and thinking. This supports the necessity of a summer break. In fact, it may be necessary to provide longer semester breaks so children have more time for their own creative pursuits.
    D. In the interests of fairness, we must consider the possibility of a longer school day.

13. Which choice best completes the sentences below?

Our energy needs are not being adequately met, and in only a few short decades, we will be unable to satisfy the growing demand._____, no one has developed a plan to address those needs. Both sides of the argument have facts, science, and history to back their claims._____, fossil fuels are widely-used and available. _____, there is a limited supply of them and they damage the environment.

    A. So it seems, Similar to other claims, However
    B. However, On one hand, On the other hand
    C. On one hand, However, Similarly
    D. Strangely, First of all, Second of all

14. Which of the following shows the correct punctuation for this quote from Richard Feynman?
    A. If you thought that science was certain—well, that is just an error on your part.
    B. If you thought that science was certain, well that is just an error on your part.
    C. If you thought that, science was certain, well, that is just an error—on your part.
    D. If you thought—that science was certain—well, that is just an error on your part.

15. Which of the following best completes the sentence?

_____ *is a kind of reaction where a small molecule of something gets added into a carbon-carbon bond.*

    A. oxidation
    B. reduction
    C. addition reaction
    D. addition polymerization

16. Which of the following words is NOT spelled correctly?
    A. complacency
    B. indissoluble
    C. indefategable
    D. voracious

17. Which of the following is essential in a concluding statement of an argument?
    A. The introduction of new points that might lead to future arguments.
    B. A summary of the issue that reinforces clearly its main points.
    C. A contradiction of the argument's main points to provide fresh perspectives.
    D. An unrelated detail that might lighten the audience's mood after a heated debate.

18. Read the sentences, and then answer the question that follows.

I often have heard arguments claiming that complete freedom of speech could lead to dangerous situations. Without complete freedom of speech, we hardly are living in a free society.

Which word would best link these sentences?
   A. However
   B. Therefore
   C. So
   D. Supposedly

19. Which of the following statements best would conclude an essay about playwright William Shakespeare?
   A. William Shakespeare died of unknown causes on April 23, 1616.
   B. William Shakespeare wrote the most important plays ever written, and I think his best one is definitely Romeo and Juliet.
   C. William Shakespeare's plays have been staged in theaters throughout the world, yet he will always be most closely associated with the Globe Theater in London.
   D. Although William Shakespeare died in 1616, the artistry and eternal relevance of his work destined it to thrive for hundreds of years into the future.

20. Read the sentences, and then answer the question that follows.

In the past, television has been criticized as a medium without the complexity and artfulness of cinema. Contemporary programs, such as "Mad Men," are widely celebrated for their intricately structured narratives and beautifully realized design.

Which of the following statements best links these sentences?
   A. Today's television shows prove that the medium has not changed much.
   B. "Mad Men" is a television show about the advertising business of the 1960s.
   C. This attitude has changed drastically over time.
   D. Television now offers a wide range of comedies, dramas, and reality shows.

21. Which version of the sentence is written correctly?
   A. A Los-Angeles-area homeowner decided to relocate to San Francisco.
   B. A Los Angeles area homeowner decided to relocate to San Francisco.
   C. A Los Angeles-area homeowner decided to relocate to San Francisco.
   D. A Los-Angeles-area-homeowner decided to relocate to San Francisco.

22. Which version of the sentence is written correctly?
   A. Please lie the porcelain vase down gently to avoid chipping it.
   B. Please lain the porcelain vase down gently to avoid chipping it.
   C. Please lies the porcelain vase down gently to avoid chipping it.
   D. Please lay the porcelain vase down gently to avoid chipping it.

23. As used in the sentence, "The beach is at its most placid at sunset, after most people have gone home," what does the word placid mean?
    A. peaceful
    B. pitiful
    C. pretty
    D. picturesque

24. Which version of the sentence does NOT contain any misspelled words?
    A. The pompouse man thought he was better than everyone else.
    B. The pompous man thought he was better than everyone else.
    C. The pompus man thought he was better than everyone else.
    D. The pompis man thought he was better than everyone else.

25. Which version of the sentence creates the best feeling of suspense?
    A. The owl pounced on the rabbit suddenly when it spied the helpless animal emerging from the brush.
    B. When the owl spied the rabbit emerging from the brush, it pounced on the helpless animal suddenly.
    C. It pounced on the helpless animal suddenly when the owl spied the rabbit emerging from the brush.
    D. Suddenly, the owl pounced on the rabbit when it spied the helpless animal emerging from the brush.

26. Which of the following choices is the best way to write the sentence?
    A. There is no way to instantly learn a new language.
    B. Instantly there is no way to learn a new language.
    C. There is no instantly way to learn a new language.
    D. There is no way to learn a new language instantly.

27. Which of the following choices best completes the passage?
    Standardized tests are becoming more important every year, and _____ these tests may seem like an easy way for educators to evaluate many students at once, there are considerable drawbacks. _____, teachers frequently teach to the test, which may raise scores but lowers the quality of education. _____: a recent survey showing that students know little information that is not tested on a standardized exam.

    A. while, for example, case in point
    B. since, while, interestingly
    C. although, consequently, moreover
    D. because, on the other hand, yet

28. Which of the following choices best completes the passage?

Genetic engineering is not just a new way of approaching the same breeding methods used by farmers for centuries. _____, it is a completely new way of dealing with living things. _____ some scientists say that we are only working with what nature has given us, this is clearly not the case. We are not working with nature, we are creating it. We are making ourselves gods.

    A. However, For example
    B. On the contrary, While
    C. Notably, Case in point
    D. First, Second

29. Which of the following sentences best completes the selection?

The flu is a common disease that plagues millions of Americans every year. Symptoms include a runny nose, fever, coughing, and an overall feeling of achiness. While there is little that can be done once someone catches the flu, there is one important step most people fail to take to prevent themselves from getting it.

    A. They don't wash their hands when they go to the bathroom.
    B. They fail to do something that is vital to protecting their health.
    C. They only wash their hands if someone is watching them.
    D. They fail to wash their hands thoroughly and frequently.

30. Which of the following is correct?
    A. Mary had said: "I believe in the rights of my fellow man."
    B. Since Fred: Jerry: and Peter wanted to go, they drove the van.
    C. The Constitution: it is one of the greatest documents of all time: it is vital to our freedom.
    D. Scientists need to keep finding new sources of money to support their research.

Answers and Explanations

Mathematics

1. A: $(y^9 \div y^3) \times 2$
Since we know that $y = 2$, it is simply a matter of substituting this value into the equation.
$(2^9 \div 2^3) \times 2$
$(512 \div 8) \times 2$
$64 \times 2 = 128$

2. C: $\dfrac{16x^3 - 32x^2 + 8x}{4x}$
To simplify, each term in the numerator can be divided by $4x$ to eliminate the denominator.
The law of exponents that indicates that $x^n/x^m = x^{n-m}$ must be observed.
We are left with: $4x^2 - 8x + 2$

3. C: $x^2 + 8x + 16 = 0$
To solve for x, simplify this equation through factoring.
$(x + 4)(x + 4) = 0$
$x + 4 = 0$
$x = -4$

4. B: $x^2 + 7x + 12$
This expression can be simplified by using factoring.
The factors are $(x + 4)(x + 3)$.
To check the answer, multiply the first, outside, inside, and last terms (FOIL).
$x^2 + 3x + 4x + 12$
Combine like terms.
$x^2 + 7x + 12$

5. D: First, compute the value enclosed by the parentheses, 3b+5= 3 x 7 + 5= 26. Next, compute 4a = -24. Note that a is negative, so that this product is negative as well. The product 4a(3b+5) will therefore be negative as well, and equals -624. Finally, add the value of 2b, or 2 x 7 =14, to -624, to get the final answer -624+14=610.

6. C: The point-slope form of an equation is $(y - y_1) = m(x - x_1)$ given slope m and a point (x_1, y_1). The problem gives the slope $m = -2$ and the point $(x_1, y_1) = (-3, 4)$.
Substitute these values into the point-slope form:
$$(y - y_1) = m(x - x_1) \rightarrow (y - 4) = -2(x - (-3))$$
Distribute the -2 and combine like terms:
$$(y - 4) = -2(x - (-3)) \rightarrow y - 4 = -2(x + 3) \rightarrow y - 4 = -2x - 6 \rightarrow y = -2x - 2$$
Do not stop here. While this is a correct equation using the given parameters, it does not satisfy the requirements of the problem. You are told to find the equation in standard form, and you have slope-intercept form. Standard form is $ax + by + c = 0$.
Rearrange the terms in your equation to fit this form:
$$y = -2x - 2 \rightarrow 2x + y + 2 = 0$$

7. B: To calculate the slope of a line, we simply have to figure out the change in y over the change in x.

$$\frac{18 - 2}{-3 - 5} = \frac{16}{-8} = -2$$

-2 is the slope of the line.

8. B: A: prime number has only two whole integer divisors, 1 and itself. This is true of 3, 17, and 41. However 6 can be divided by 1, 2, 3, and 6. It is therefore not a prime number.

9. D: Since $4^3 = 4 \times 4 \times 4 = 64$, and $3^4 = 3 \times 3 \times 3 \times 3 = 81$, the answer is $81 - 64 = 17$.

10. D: To find a midpoint, simply calculate the average of the two sets of points.
For x, the midpoint is calculated in the following manner:
(-20 + 5)/2 = -7.5
For y, the midpoint is calculated in the following manner:
(8 + 3)/2 = 5.5
The midpoint is (-7.5, 5.5)

11. D: $x^5 x^2 + y^0 =$
We know that $x = 3$.
Therefore, we can find the value of $x^5 x^2$
$3^5 3^2$
$243 \cdot 9 = 2{,}187$
We don't know the value of y, but any value to the power of zero is equal to one.
Therefore, $2{,}187 + 1 = 2{,}188$

12. A: Since we know the value of x and y, it is simply a matter of substituting them into the expression:
$9x - 3y + 8xy - 3$
$9(10) - 3(-2) + 8(10)(-2) - 3$
$90 + 6 - 160 - 3$
$96 - 163 = -67$

13. B: $9x (3x^2 + 2x - 9)$
To simplify, multiply the value outside of the brackets ($9x$) by the values inside of the brackets.
$9x \cdot 3x^2 + 9x \cdot 2x - 9x \cdot 9$
$27x^3 + 18 x^2 - 81x$

14. A: $(2x - 5)(x+7)$
To expand, multiply the first terms, outside terms, inside terms, and then the last terms (FOIL)
$2x^2 + 14x - 5x - 35$
Combine like terms.
$2x^2 + 9x - 35$

15. B: To evaluate the expression for the given values of x and y, substitute the values into the expression and then calculate the result:
$$2x^2 + 5x - y^2 = 2(3)^2 + 5(3) - (5)^2$$
$$= 2 \cdot 9 + 5 \cdot 3 - 25$$
$$= 18 + 15 - 25$$
$$= 8$$

16. A: To add quadratic expressions, combine like terms. In this problem, there are three sets of like terms: the y^2-terms, the y-terms, and the constants. Set up the addition vertically, making sure to line up like terms, and then add them together:

$$\begin{array}{r} y^2 + 9y - 2 \\ + \ 4y^2 - y - 5 \\ \hline 5y^2 + 8y - 7 \end{array}$$

17. B: The given equation is a quadratic equation that can be solved by factorization. First, move everything to one side to get it in the correct form, by subtracting 6 from both sides:
$$x^2 + 5x = 6$$
$$x^2 + 5x - 6 = 0$$
This factors out to:
$$(x + 6)(x - 1) = 0$$
Thus, the two solutions to the equation are $x = -6$ and $x = 1$.

18. C: A percent is a part divided by the whole $\left(\frac{\text{part}}{\text{whole}}\right)$. In this problem, the part is 42 and the whole is 56, so the ratio can be expressed as $\frac{42}{56}$, or 0.75:
$$\frac{42}{56} = 0.75 = 75\%$$

19. D: First convert the percent to a decimal number by dividing it by 100, or, equivalently, by moving the decimal point two places to the left:
$$56\% = 0.56$$
Next, calculate 56% of 25 by multiplying 25 by 0.56:
$$0.56 \times 25 = 14$$

20. B: $5 \times (80 / 8) + (7 - 2) - (9 \times 5) =$
Remember the order of operations: Parentheses, exponents, multiplication, division, addition, subtraction.
Perform the operations inside the parentheses first:
$5 \times (10) + (5) - (45) =$
Then, do any multiplication and division, working from left to right:
$50 + 5 - 45 =$
Finally, do any adding or subtracting, working from left to right:
$55 - 45 = 10$

21. B: According to the order of operations (PEMDAS), first simplify the numerator and the denominator of the expression, then perform the division:
$$\frac{4 - (-12)}{-9 + 5} = \frac{4 + 12}{-9 + 5} = \frac{16}{-4} = -4$$

22. C: The given equations form a system of linear equations. Since the first equation is already given in terms of x, it will be easier to solve it using the substitution method. Start by substituting $2y - 3$ for x in the second equation:

$$2x + \frac{1}{2}y = 3 \qquad 2(2y - 3) + \frac{1}{2}y = 3$$

Next, solve the resulting equation for y. Distribute the 2 and then combine like y-terms in the result:

$$4y - 6 + \frac{1}{2}y = 3 \qquad \frac{9}{2}y - 6 = 3$$

Finally, isolate the variable y by adding 6 to both sides and then dividing both sides by the coefficient of y, which is $\frac{9}{2}$ (or, equivalently, multiply by 2 and divide by 9):

$$\frac{9}{2}y = 9 \qquad y = 2$$

23. A: $2x - 6y = 12$
$\qquad -6x + 14y = 42$

To solve a variable using a system of equations, one of the variables must be cancelled out. To eliminate x from these equations, first multiply the top equation by 3.
$3(2x - 6y = 12)$
$6x - 18y = 36$
Then, add the two equations to eliminate x.
$\qquad 6x - 18y = 36$
$\underline{+ \ -6x + 14y = 42}$
$\qquad\qquad -4y = 78$
Solve for y.
$-4y = 78$
$y = 78/-4$
$y = -19.5$

24. A: Use the first equation to solve for x.
$6x + 2x - 26 = -5x$
$8x + 5x = 26$
$13x = 26$
$x = 2$
Then, evaluate the second equation.
$[(2x - 1)/7]^3$
$[(2 \times 2 - 1)/7]^3$
$[3/7]^3$
$[0.4285]^3$
$= 0.0787$
Rounding, we get 0.08

25. B: To solve, first do the multiplication on each side of the equation: $3x + 42 = 4x + 36$. Then get like terms on opposite sides of the equation: $x = 6$

26. B: The evaluation of the equation, for an x-value of -2, gives the following: $y = \frac{(-2)^4 - 2}{(-2)^2 + 1}$, which reduces to $y = \frac{16 - 2}{4 + 1}$, or $y = \frac{14}{5}$. The improper fraction, $\frac{14}{5}$, can also be written as the mixed number, $2\frac{4}{5}$. Thus, $y = 2\frac{4}{5}$.

27. D: The polynomial can be factored as $(x-7)(x+3)$. Thus, $(x-7)$ is a factor of the given polynomial.

28. C: The linear equation can be rewritten as $y = -\frac{2}{3}x + \frac{7}{3}$. The slope-intercept form of an equation, or $y = mx + b$, includes m as the slope and b as the y-intercept. Therefore, the y-intercept of the equation is $\frac{7}{3}$.

29. D: When dividing terms with identical bases, the exponents are to be subtracted, i.e., $\frac{a^4}{a^3} = a^1$ or a. Thus, the rational expression can be rewritten $a^{11}b^{-15}c^{-2}$. The rules of exponents also state: $a^{-x} = \frac{1}{a^x}$. So, the rational expression can now be rewritten as $\frac{a^{11}}{b^{15}c^2}$.

30. D: The radical expression can be rewritten as the product, $\sqrt[3]{8x^3y^6}\sqrt[3]{x^2y}$, which simplifies to $2xy^2\sqrt[3]{x^2y}$. This product can be rewritten as $2xy^2(x^2y)^{\frac{1}{3}}$, or $2xy^2\left(x^{\frac{2}{3}}y^{\frac{1}{3}}\right)$. Multiplying the two expressions gives $2x^{\frac{5}{3}}y^{\frac{7}{3}}$.

Reading

1. B. The passage gives general instructions for tomato plant culture from seeding to providing support for the vines. Answers A and D are too specific, focusing on details of the text. Answer C is too general: the passage does not fully describe how to operate a farm.

2. A. The passage states that seeds germinated in late March will be ready for the garden after the last frost, implying that exposure to freezing temperatures would harm them.

3. A. The text states that pinching the bud is done to make the plants stronger.

4. A. The text states that use of fresh manure will delay fruiting.

5. D. Although all the other answers make mention of information contained in the paragraph, the overall purpose of this paragraph is as stated, to describe the support procedure.

6. D. At first repelled by the sight of Garth in the window, the girl eventually expresses pity when she learns that he is deaf, too.

7. D. When he lifted his supplicating eye, it was referring to the way that he was begging. He was giving her a begging look and then stopped.

8. C. Garth is sad that he is so deformed that other people are frequently repelled and try to avoid contact with him.

9. A. Despite his ugliness and deformity, Garth is a gentle soul who wants to be accepted as a friend by the girl.

10. B. In the first sentence the phrase "so long had sleep been denied her" tells us she had been prevented from sleeping for some time.

11. B. This question is concerned with the main idea of the passage. Although the passage is not explicit about why Martin and Beth's relationship is strained, by eliminating a number of answer choices, the right answer can easily be found. Choice A can be eliminated because Martin has not lost his job—he receives a page at the end of the passage concerning one of his patients. Choice B is not contradicted by the passage, but all that the reader is told is that Martin and Mary were once together. Choice C can be eliminated because the passage does not indicate how much Martin works. Choice D can be eliminated because Martin tells Beth that if she wants to go to the movies, they can go. The best choice, then, is B.

12. D: This question asks for the definition of "fine" within the passage. "Fine" can mean "good," "precious," or "sharp," but this question asks for the meaning of "fine" within the passage itself. Choices A and B are inappropriate because Beth says that "fine" used to mean these things but does not any longer. Choice C is inappropriate for the same reason: while "fine" can mean "very good" or "sharp," it does not mean these things within the passage. Choice D is the best answer because Beth says "fine" is "a meaningless word, an excuse not to tell other people what's on your mind." Even though "fine" can mean choices A–C, the question asks what "fine" means according to Beth. Thus, the best choice is D.

13. A: This question asks for the best definition of "rapport." A "rapport" is a relationship based on mutual understanding. With this in mind, Choice A might be a good answer, even though it is not an exact match. Choice B can be eliminated because it does not describe a relationship. Choice C can be eliminated because individuals can have a relationship based on mutual understanding without sharing a common goal. Choice D can be eliminated because loneliness or boredom have nothing to do with the definition of "rapport."

14. B: This question asks the reader to make a conclusion based on details from the passage. The reader knows that (1) Martin wears a pager for his job, (2) he has patients, and (3) one of his patients is going into cardiac arrest. Choices A and D can be eliminated because mechanics, film directors, and television producers do not see patients. Choice C seems like a possibility. After all, dentists see patients. Choice B is the best choice because if a person goes into cardiac arrest it is more likely a medical doctor rather than a dentist would be paged.

15. C: This question asks the reader to make an inference about what is going to happen based on the passage. Choice A is inappropriate because the passage says nothing about Martin's level of satisfaction with his job. Choice B is can be eliminated for a similar reason—the passage says nothing about Beth's desire for children. Choice C seems like a good choice because while Martin tells Beth he has to leave to go to work, the structure of the sentence immediately preceding this makes it seem as if Beth knows Martin is going to leave her: "Beth wasn't even sure she knew Martin anymore, but she was confident that it was only a matter of time before everything was not "fine," only a matter of time before he told her…" Choice D is inappropriate because there is nothing in the passage that indicates how long Beth and Martin have known each other. The best choice, then, is C.

16. C. An archipelago is a large group or chain of islands.

17. D. The article deals primarily with the ways the colonists fed themselves: their crops and the foods they hunted. While it also describes New Zealand's prehistory, the main focus is on food sources.

18. B. The article states that the islands were colonized by Polynesians in the fifteenth century but that the first settlers had arrived some 400 years earlier than that.

19. C. The sweet potato could be stored, providing a source of food during the winter when other food gathering activities were difficult.

20. A. The sweet potato provided a winter food source through storage, allowing the population to increase.

21. D. The moa were flightless birds, so they could not easily escape when the humans came to hunt them.

22. D. The passage states that the first settlers were forced to rely on fishing for their food.

23. C: The first paragraph states that the main purpose of DST it to make better use of daylight.

24. A: Energy conservation is discussed as a possible benefit of DST, not a negative effect of it.

25. D: The first paragraph states that DST involves setting clocks forward one hour in the spring and one hour backward in the fall.

26. B: The last sentence in paragraph four notes that agricultural and evening entertainment interests have historically been opposed to DST.

27. D: The passage gives examples of both good and bad effects extra daylight can have on health.

28. C: The last paragraph of the passage notes that DST can lead to peculiar situations, and relays an anecdote about the effect of DST on the birth order of twins.

29. B: In the second paragraph, the author asserts that Benjamin Franklin suggested DST as a way to save candles.

30. D: The sixth paragraph notes that DST is observed in only some regions of Brazil.

Writing

1. B: The word *fourth* should be written out to match the form of *third.* While the word *teacher* could become plural, choice A is incorrect because the second sentence of the passage shows that Alberto is talking about a single teacher. Choice C is incorrect because the comma correctly separates two independent clauses. Choice D is incorrect because

Alberto is talking about several years rather than the possessive of one year. Therefore, the form of *years* should be plural rather than possessive.

2. D: The correct answer is Choice D because it uses proper word order to get the point across. Choice D begins with a subject and verb and follows the verb by two objects. Choice A is incorrect because the phrases *my teacher to hate me back* and *for me to hate him* are written in reverse order. It is more logical for *for me to hate him* to be written first. Choice B is incorrect because the subject and verb separate Alberto's two emotions (*expecting to hate my teacher* and *expecting him to hate me back*). This separation makes the sentence more difficult to read and understand. Choice C is incorrect because Alberto states twice that he expected to hate Mr. Shanbourne.

3. C: The correct answer is Choice C because the word *because* combines the sentence by showing that the second clause is an explanation for the first clause. Choice A is incorrect because the conjunction *and* doesn't show how the two clauses are connected. Choice B is incorrect because the word *although* doesn't logically connect the two clauses. The word *although* implies that the two clauses contradict each other; instead, the second clause explains the first. Although *as a result of* has a similar meaning to *because* and could be used to effectively combine the sentences, choice D is incorrect because the verbs *forced* and *gave* should be changed to *forcing* and *giving* in order for *as a result of* to be used correctly.

4. C: The phrase *handed in assignments after the due date* is redundant with the phrase *turned in work late*; only one of those phrases needs to be in the sentence. Choices A and B are incorrect because both phrases add unique information to the sentence. Choice D is incorrect because the sentence has two redundant phrases, and one of them should be deleted.

5. D: This transition word shows that Mr. Shanbourne waited for a while and then decided to talk to Alberto about his behavior. Choice A is incorrect because the word *however* implies that the following sentence will contradict what came before. Instead, sentence 16 is a culmination of Alberto's behavior. Choice B is incorrect because the word *actually* is also a transition used to show a contrast between the two sentences. *Eventually* is a better transition word because it shows that the sentences are sequentially related. Choice C is incorrect because *furthermore* implies that the following sentence will present additional proof about a point.

6. A: perceive. This is the correct form of the word for the sentence.

7. A: concoct. While the words are all very similar in meaning (denotation), only *concoct* best matches the tone of the passage: Emil is prone to developing wild ideas that result in disaster. "Invent" (B) and "design" (D) have positive connotations, while "make" (C) has a neutral feeling about it.

8. C: Although Biraju was not an accident-prone person, he knew that his older brother did not share this trait. Only choice C correctly uses the hyphen. Hyphens are used for many reasons, such as to make an adjective and a noun a compound word or in numbers (fifty-seven). Choice A uses too many hyphens (real-estate-broker), B does not use "easy-to-remember" as an adjective, and D is missing hyphens "twenty-one-year-old students".

9. B: paroxysm. A paroxysm is a fit or sudden attack of a disease or emotion.

10. B: reception. The sentence clearly requires a noun. In this case, "reception" is the only word that correctly completes the sentence.

11. A: Increasing the money supply may serve temporarily to boost the economy, but such an action damages the value of the dollar in the long run. This is the only argument supporting the idea that printing money may not be the best option. Expansionary monetary policy refers to the government action of increasing the money supply. The other choices do not address this policy directly.

12. C: The limitations of this view are clear: there are no scientifically-backed works establishing that students perform better if they spend more time in school. However, there is significant research establishing the idea that learners do require time for creative pursuits and thinking. This supports the necessity of a summer break. In fact, it may be necessary to provide longer semester breaks so children have more time for their own creative pursuits. Only this choice develops and supports a counterclaim. Choice A provides a counterclaim but does not give support. Choice B does not address the claim. Choice D actually supports the claim, and adds on the issue of teacher salaries.

13. B: However, On one hand, On the other hand
This is the best choice because the first blank shows a change in the direction. The second blank is part of a sentence indicating that an initial point will be made. The final blank is in a sentence that indicates a contradiction has occurred.

14. A: If you thought that science was certain—well, that is just an error on your part. This choice is the only one that is punctuated correctly. All of the other choices show incorrect ways of expressing the sentence.

15. C: addition reaction. This choice completes the sentence with the correct vocabulary. An addition reaction occurs when a smaller molecule is added into a double (or sometimes triple) carbon bond. Choice A is oxidation, which happens when a substance loses electrons. Choice B is reduction, which happens when a substance gains electrons, and Choice D refers to the joining of monomers.

16. C: indefategable. This word is spelled incorrectly; it should be "indefatigable." The other words are all correct.

17. B: The key to an effective concluding statement is a concise summary of the argument's main points. Such a conclusion leaves the opponent and audience with a clear and organized understanding of the argument. The introduction of new points or a detail merely added to lighten mood would weaken the argument by straying off point at the last minute. Introducing contradictory perspectives completely would work against the argument's effectiveness.

18. A: The first sentence introduces an argument against complete freedom of speech. The second sentence makes an argument in favor of it. The second sentence contradicts the first one, so the two sentences should be linked with the adverb "however." "Therefore" and "so" would be used only if the sentences supported each other.

19. D: This statement mentions the death of William Shakespeare, effectively indicating his end. It also refers to the importance of his work and the continued relevance of his work in the years to come, which is integral to any general essay about the playwright. This statement offers a stronger conclusion to an essay on William Shakespeare than stopping short with the cause and date of his death. In addition, this choice does not stray from an authoritative tone by presenting personal opinion about Shakespeare's best play or a random detail about the theaters that staged his work.

20. C: The first sentence explains how television once was criticized. The second sentence shows how contemporary shows now are being praised. They require a linking sentence indicating that an attitude change toward television has occurred over time. Explaining the premise of "Mad Men" or the variety of shows on television does not address the best way to link these sentences. Stating, "Today's television shows prove that the medium has not changed much," contradicts the second sentence.

21. C: A compound modifier consists of more than two words, which must be linked with one or more hyphen in order to be correct. In this sentence, "Los Angeles-homeowner" is a compound modifier. Although "Los Angeles" consists of two words, it is a single city name and does not require a hyphen between "Los" and "Angeles."

22. D: The words lie and lay often are confused, but they are not used in the same way. Lie means to recline, as a person might lie on a bed. Lay is a verb meaning to place an object. Since a porcelain vase is an object, the correct word is lay in this sentence.

23. A: Although the words pretty and picturesque make sense in the context of this sentence, it contains clues indicating a more accurate answer choice. When people leave an area, they take their noise and activities with them, leaving the place relatively peaceful. A beach would be at its most peaceful after people have left it after sunset. Based on this context, you can conclude that placid and peaceful have the same meaning.

24. B: The word pompous, meaning arrogant or self-important, is spelled with an "ou," creating an "uh" sound.

25. B: Although all of these sentences technically are correct, only choice B uses syntax to establish a feeling of suspense. It achieves this by saving the action—the owl pouncing on the rabbit—for the end of the sentence. The other answer choices give away the action right away.

26. D: Choices B and C clearly misuse the adverb "instantly" by placing it where it does not make sense. Choice A is more of a grey area. Placing "instantly" inside the phrase "to learn" creates a split infinitive. Technically, a split infinitive is a form of incorrect grammar, yet it has become so widely used that many people now accept it as correct. However, it remains technically incorrect, and choice D is the best answer choice.

27. A: while, for example, case in point
This is the best choice for this passage because an idea is introduced, and then there is a change in the direction. The change in direction acknowledges another point of view. The next sentence illustrates part of the author's argument with a supporting idea (standardized tests lower the quality of education). The last sentence is talking about a specific example and using the colon to break up the sentence.

28. B: On the contrary, While

The transitions needed here must complete the sentences while preserving the direction of the passage. The first sentence gives us one direction, then the second sentence provides a contradiction. The third sentence is about what scientists are saying, but includes a contrasting comment.

29. D: They fail to wash their hands thoroughly and frequently.

This is the only choice that matches the style and tone of the passage. Choices A and C are too informal. Choice B does not complete the passage.

30. A: Mary had said: "I believe in the rights of my fellow man."

This is the only choice that uses the colon correctly; it introduces a quotation. The other choices do not use the colon in the correct way to introduce either a quotation or a list of items.

Secret Key #1 - Guessing is not Guesswork

You probably know that guessing is a good idea - unlike other standardized tests, there is no penalty for getting a wrong answer. Even if you have no idea about a question, you still have a 20-25% chance of getting it right.

Most test takers do not understand the impact that proper guessing can have on their score. Unless you score extremely high, guessing will significantly contribute to your final score.

Monkeys Take the Test

What most test takers don't realize is that to insure that 20-25% chance, you have to guess randomly. If you put 20 monkeys in a room to take this test, assuming they answered once per question and behaved themselves, on average they would get 20-25% of the questions correct. Put 20 test takers in the room, and the average will be much lower among guessed questions. Why?

1. The test writers intentionally write deceptive answer choices that "look" right. A test taker has no idea about a question, so picks the "best looking" answer, which is often wrong. The monkey has no idea what looks good and what doesn't, so will consistently be lucky about 20-25% of the time.

2. Test takers will eliminate answer choices from the guessing pool based on a hunch or intuition. Simple but correct answers often get excluded, leaving a 0% chance of being correct. The monkey has no clue, and often gets lucky with the best choice.

This is why the process of elimination endorsed by most test courses is flawed and detrimental to your performance- test takers don't guess, they make an ignorant stab in the dark that is usually worse than random.

$5 Challenge

Let me introduce one of the most valuable ideas of this course- the $5 challenge:

You only mark your "best guess" if you are willing to bet $5 on it.
You only eliminate choices from guessing if you are willing to bet $5 on it.

Why $5? Five dollars is an amount of money that is small yet not insignificant, and can really add up fast (20 questions could cost you $100). Likewise, each answer choice on one question of the test will have a small impact on your overall score, but it can really add up to a lot of points in the end.

The process of elimination IS valuable. The following shows your chance of guessing it right:

If you eliminate wrong answer choices until only this many remain:	Chance of getting it correct:
1	100%
2	50%
3	33%

However, if you accidentally eliminate the right answer or go on a hunch for an incorrect answer, your chances drop dramatically: to 0%. By guessing among all the answer choices, you are GUARANTEED to have a shot at the right answer.

That's why the $5 test is so valuable- if you give up the advantage and safety of a pure guess, it had better be worth the risk.

What we still haven't covered is how to be sure that whatever guess you make is truly random. Here's the easiest way:

Always pick the first answer choice among those remaining.

Such a technique means that you have decided, **before you see a single test question**, exactly how you are going to guess- and since the order of choices tells you nothing about which one is correct, this guessing technique is perfectly random.

This section is not meant to scare you away from making educated guesses or eliminating choices- you just need to define when a choice is worth eliminating. The $5 test, along with a pre-defined random guessing strategy, is the best way to make sure you reap all of the benefits of guessing.

Secret Key #2 - Prepare, Don't Procrastinate

Let me state an obvious fact: if you take the test three times, you will get three different scores. This is due to the way you feel on test day, the level of preparedness you have, and, despite the test writers' claims to the contrary, some tests WILL be easier for you than others.

Since your future depends so much on your score, you should maximize your chances of success. In order to maximize the likelihood of success, you've got to prepare in advance. This means taking practice tests and spending time learning the information and test taking strategies you will need to succeed.

Never take the test as a "practice" test, expecting that you can just take it again if you need to. Feel free to take sample tests on your own, but when you go to take the official test, be prepared, be focused, and do your best the first time!

Secret Key #3 - Test Yourself

Everyone knows that time is money. There is no need to spend too much of your time or too little of your time preparing for the test. You should only spend as much of your precious time preparing as is necessary for you to get the score you need.

Once you have taken a practice test under real conditions of time constraints, then you will know if you are ready for the test or not.

If you have scored extremely high the first time that you take the practice test, then there is not much point in spending countless hours studying. You are already there.

Benchmark your abilities by retaking practice tests and seeing how much you have improved. Once you score high enough to guarantee success, then you are ready.

If you have scored well below where you need, then knuckle down and begin studying in earnest. Check your improvement regularly through the use of practice tests under real conditions. Above all, don't worry, panic, or give up. The key is perseverance!

Then, when you go to take the test, remain confident and remember how well you did on the practice tests. If you can score high enough on a practice test, then you can do the same on the real thing.

General Strategies

The most important thing you can do is to ignore your fears and jump into the test immediately- do not be overwhelmed by any strange-sounding terms. You have to jump into the test like jumping into a pool- all at once is the easiest way.

Make Predictions

As you read and understand the question, try to guess what the answer will be. Remember that several of the answer choices are wrong, and once you begin reading them, your mind will immediately become cluttered with answer choices designed to throw you off. Your mind is typically the most focused immediately after you have read the question and digested its contents. If you can, try to predict what the correct answer will be. You may be surprised at what you can predict.

Quickly scan the choices and see if your prediction is in the listed answer choices. If it is, then you can be quite confident that you have the right answer. It still won't hurt to check the other answer choices, but most of the time, you've got it!

Answer the Question

It may seem obvious to only pick answer choices that answer the question, but the test writers can create some excellent answer choices that are wrong. Don't pick an answer just because it sounds right, or you believe it to be true. It MUST answer the question. Once you've made your selection, always go back and check it against the question and make sure that you didn't misread the question, and the answer choice does answer the question posed.

Benchmark

After you read the first answer choice, decide if you think it sounds correct or not. If it doesn't, move on to the next answer choice. If it does, mentally mark that answer choice. This doesn't mean that you've definitely selected it as your answer choice, it just means that it's the best you've seen thus far. Go ahead and read the next choice. If the next choice is worse than the one you've already selected, keep going to the next answer choice. If the next choice is better than the choice you've already selected, mentally mark the new answer choice as your best guess.

The first answer choice that you select becomes your standard. Every other answer choice must be benchmarked against that standard. That choice is correct until proven otherwise by another answer choice beating it out. Once you've decided that no other answer choice seems as good, do one final check to ensure that your answer choice answers the question posed.

Valid Information

Don't discount any of the information provided in the question. Every piece of information may be necessary to determine the correct answer. None of the information in the question is there to throw you off (while the answer choices will certainly have information to throw you off). If two seemingly unrelated topics are discussed, don't ignore either. You can be confident there is a relationship, or it wouldn't be included in the question, and you are probably going to have to determine what is that relationship to find the answer.

Avoid "Fact Traps"

Don't get distracted by a choice that is factually true. Your search is for the answer that answers the question. Stay focused and don't fall for an answer that is true but incorrect. Always go back to the question and make sure you're choosing an answer that actually answers the question and is not just a true statement. An answer can be factually correct, but it MUST answer the question asked. Additionally, two answers can both be seemingly correct, so be sure to read all of the answer choices, and make sure that you get the one that BEST answers the question.

Milk the Question

Some of the questions may throw you completely off. They might deal with a subject you have not been exposed to, or one that you haven't reviewed in years. While your lack of knowledge about the subject will be a hindrance, the question itself can give you many clues that will help you find the correct answer. Read the question carefully and look for clues.

Watch particularly for adjectives and nouns describing difficult terms or words that you don't recognize. Regardless of if you completely understand a word or not, replacing it with a synonym either provided or one you more familiar with may help you to understand what the questions are asking. Rather than wracking your mind about specific detailed information concerning a difficult term or word, try to use mental substitutes that are easier to understand.

The Trap of Familiarity

Don't just choose a word because you recognize it. On difficult questions, you may not recognize a number of words in the answer choices. The test writers don't put "make-believe" words on the test; so don't think that just because you only recognize all the words in one answer choice means that answer choice must be correct. If you only recognize words in one answer choice, then focus on that one. Is it correct? Try your best to determine if it is correct. If it is, that is great, but if it doesn't, eliminate it. Each word and answer choice you eliminate increases your chances of getting the question correct, even if you then have to guess among the unfamiliar choices.

Eliminate Answers

Eliminate choices as soon as you realize they are wrong. But be careful! Make sure you consider all of the possible answer choices. Just because one appears right, doesn't mean that the next one won't be even better! The test writers will usually put more than one good answer choice for every question, so read all of them. Don't worry if you are stuck between two that seem right. By getting down to just two remaining possible choices, your odds are now 50/50. Rather than wasting too much time, play the odds. You are guessing, but guessing wisely, because you've been able to knock out some of the answer choices that you know are wrong. If you are eliminating choices and realize that the last answer choice you are left with is also obviously wrong, don't panic. Start over and consider each choice again. There may easily be something that you missed the first time and will realize on the second pass.

Tough Questions

If you are stumped on a problem or it appears too hard or too difficult, don't waste time. Move on! Remember though, if you can quickly check for obviously incorrect answer choices, your chances of guessing correctly are greatly improved. Before you completely give up, at least try to knock out a couple of possible answers. Eliminate what you can and then guess at the remaining answer choices before moving on.

Brainstorm

If you get stuck on a difficult question, spend a few seconds quickly brainstorming. Run through the complete list of possible answer choices. Look at each choice and ask yourself, "Could this answer the question satisfactorily?" Go through each answer choice and consider it independently of the other. By systematically going through all possibilities, you may find something that you would otherwise overlook. Remember that when you get stuck, it's important to try to keep moving.

Read Carefully

Understand the problem. Read the question and answer choices carefully. Don't miss the question because you misread the terms. You have plenty of time to read each question thoroughly and make sure you understand what is being asked. Yet a happy medium must be attained, so don't waste too much time. You must read carefully, but efficiently.

Face Value

When in doubt, use common sense. Always accept the situation in the problem at face value. Don't read too much into it. These problems will not require you to make huge leaps of logic. The test writers aren't trying to throw you off with a cheap trick. If you have to go beyond creativity and make a leap of logic in order to have an answer choice answer the question, then you should look at the other answer choices. Don't overcomplicate the problem by creating theoretical relationships or explanations that will warp time or space. These are normal problems rooted in reality. It's just that the applicable relationship or explanation may not be readily apparent and you have to figure things out. Use your common sense to interpret anything that isn't clear.

Prefixes

If you're having trouble with a word in the question or answer choices, try dissecting it. Take advantage of every clue that the word might include. Prefixes and suffixes can be a huge help. Usually they allow you to determine a basic meaning. Pre- means before, post- means after, pro - is positive, de- is negative. From these prefixes and suffixes, you can get an idea of the general meaning of the word and try to put it into context. Beware though of any traps. Just because con is the opposite of pro, doesn't necessarily mean congress is the opposite of progress!

Hedge Phrases

Watch out for critical "hedge" phrases, such as likely, may, can, will often, sometimes, often, almost, mostly, usually, generally, rarely, sometimes. Question writers insert these hedge phrases to cover every possibility. Often an answer choice will be wrong simply because it leaves no room for exception. Avoid answer choices that have definitive words like "exactly," and "always".

Switchback Words

Stay alert for "switchbacks". These are the words and phrases frequently used to alert you to shifts in thought. The most common switchback word is "but". Others include although, however, nevertheless, on the other hand, even though, while, in spite of, despite, regardless of.

New Information

Correct answer choices will rarely have completely new information included. Answer choices typically are straightforward reflections of the material asked about and will directly relate to the question. If a new piece of information is included in an answer choice that doesn't even seem to relate to the topic being asked about, then that answer choice is likely incorrect. All of the information needed to answer the question is usually provided for you, and so you should not have to make guesses that are unsupported or choose answer choices that require unknown information that cannot be reasoned on its own.

Time Management

On technical questions, don't get lost on the technical terms. Don't spend too much time on any one question. If you don't know what a term means, then since you don't have a dictionary, odds are you aren't going to get much further. You should immediately recognize terms as whether or not you know them. If you don't, work with the other clues that you have, the other answer choices and terms provided, but don't waste too much time trying to figure out a difficult term.

Contextual Clues

Look for contextual clues. An answer can be right but not correct. The contextual clues will help you find the answer that is most right and is correct. Understand the context in which a phrase or statement is made. This will help you make important distinctions.

Don't Panic

Panicking will not answer any questions for you. Therefore, it isn't helpful. When you first see the question, if your mind goes blank, take a deep breath. Force yourself to mechanically go through the steps of solving the problem and using the strategies you've learned.

Pace Yourself

Don't get clock fever. It's easy to be overwhelmed when you're looking at a page full of questions, your mind is full of random thoughts and feeling confused, and the clock is ticking down faster than you would like. Calm down and maintain the pace that you have set for yourself. As long as you are on track by monitoring your pace, you are guaranteed to have enough time for yourself. When you get to the last few minutes of the test, it may seem like you won't have enough time left, but if you only have as many questions as you should have left at that point, then you're right on track!

Answer Selection

The best way to pick an answer choice is to eliminate all of those that are wrong, until only one is left and confirm that is the correct answer. Sometimes though, an answer choice may immediately look right. Be careful! Take a second to make sure that the other choices are not equally obvious. Don't make a hasty mistake. There are only two times that you should stop before checking other answers. First is when you are positive that the answer choice you have selected is correct. Second is when time is almost out and you have to make a quick guess!

Check Your Work

Since you will probably not know every term listed and the answer to every question, it is important that you get credit for the ones that you do know. Don't miss any questions through careless mistakes. If at all possible, try to take a second to look back over your answer selection and make sure you've selected the correct answer choice and haven't made a costly careless mistake (such as marking an answer choice that you didn't mean to mark). This quick double check should more than pay for itself in caught mistakes for the time it costs.

Beware of Directly Quoted Answers

Sometimes an answer choice will repeat word for word a portion of the question or reference section. However, beware of such exact duplication – it may be a trap! More than likely, the correct choice will paraphrase or summarize a point, rather than being exactly the same wording.

Slang

Scientific sounding answers are better than slang ones. An answer choice that begins "To compare the outcomes…" is much more likely to be correct than one that begins "Because some people insisted…"

Extreme Statements

Avoid wild answers that throw out highly controversial ideas that are proclaimed as established fact. An answer choice that states the "process should be used in certain situations, if…" is much more likely to be correct than one that states the "process should be discontinued completely." The first is a calm rational statement and doesn't even make a definitive, uncompromising stance, using a hedge word "if" to provide wiggle room, whereas the second choice is a radical idea and far more extreme.

Answer Choice Families

When you have two or more answer choices that are direct opposites or parallels, one of them is usually the correct answer. For instance, if one answer choice states "x increases" and another answer choice states "x decreases" or "y increases," then those two or three answer choices are very similar in construction and fall into the same family of answer choices. A family of answer choices is when two or three answer choices are very similar in construction, and yet often have a directly opposite meaning. Usually the correct answer choice will be in that family of answer choices. The "odd man out" or answer choice that doesn't seem to fit the parallel construction of the other answer choices is more likely to be incorrect.

Special Report: How to Overcome Test Anxiety

The very nature of tests caters to some level of anxiety, nervousness or tension, just as we feel for any important event that occurs in our lives. A little bit of anxiety or nervousness can be a good thing. It helps us with motivation, and makes achievement just that much sweeter. However, too much anxiety can be a problem; especially if it hinders our ability to function and perform.

"Test anxiety," is the term that refers to the emotional reactions that some test-takers experience when faced with a test or exam. Having a fear of testing and exams is based upon a rational fear, since the test-taker's performance can shape the course of an academic career. Nevertheless, experiencing excessive fear of examinations will only interfere with the test-takers ability to perform, and his/her chances to be successful.

There are a large variety of causes that can contribute to the development and sensation of test anxiety. These include, but are not limited to lack of performance and worrying about issues surrounding the test.

Lack of Preparation

Lack of preparation can be identified by the following behaviors or situations:
- Not scheduling enough time to study, and therefore cramming the night before the test or exam
- Managing time poorly, to create the sensation that there is not enough time to do everything
- Failing to organize the text information in advance, so that the study material consists of the entire text and not simply the pertinent information
- Poor overall studying habits

Worrying, on the other hand, can be related to both the test taker, or many other factors around him/her that will be affected by the results of the test. These include worrying about:

- Previous performances on similar exams, or exams in general
- How friends and other students are achieving
- The negative consequences that will result from a poor grade or failure

There are three primary elements to test anxiety. Physical components, which involve the same typical bodily reactions as those to acute anxiety (to be discussed below). Emotional factors have to do with fear or panic. Mental or cognitive issues concerning attention spans and memory abilities.

Physical Signals

There are many different symptoms of test anxiety, and these are not limited to mental and emotional strain. Frequently there are a range of physical signals that will let a test taker know that he/she is suffering from test anxiety. These bodily changes can include the following:

- Perspiring
- Sweaty palms
- Wet, trembling hands
- Nausea
- Dry mouth
- A knot in the stomach
- Headache
- Faintness
- Muscle tension
- Aching shoulders, back and neck
- Rapid heart beat
- Feeling too hot/cold

To recognize the sensation of test anxiety, a test-taker should monitor him/herself for the following sensations:

- The physical distress symptoms as listed above
- Emotional sensitivity, expressing emotional feelings such as the need to cry or laugh too much, or a sensation of anger or helplessness
- A decreased ability to think, causing the test-taker to blank out or have racing thoughts that are hard to organize or control.

Though most students will feel some level of anxiety when faced with a test or exam, the majority can cope with that anxiety and maintain it at a manageable level. However, those who cannot are faced with a very real and very serious condition, which can and should be controlled for the immeasurable benefit of this sufferer.

Naturally, these sensations lead to negative results for the testing experience. The most common effects of test anxiety have to do with nervousness and mental blocking.

Nervousness

Nervousness can appear in several different levels:

- The test-taker's difficulty, or even inability to read and understand the questions on the test
- The difficulty or inability to organize thoughts to a coherent form
- The difficulty or inability to recall key words and concepts relating to the testing questions (especially essays)
- The receipt of poor grades on a test, though the test material was well known by the test taker

Conversely, a person may also experience mental blocking, which involves:

- Blanking out on test questions
- Only remembering the correct answers to the questions when the test has already finished.

Fortunately for test anxiety sufferers, beating these feelings, to a large degree, has to do with proper preparation. When a test taker has a feeling of preparedness, then anxiety will be dramatically lessened.

The first step to resolving anxiety issues is to distinguish which of the two types of anxiety are being suffered. If the anxiety is a direct result of a lack of preparation, this should be considered a normal reaction, and the anxiety level (as opposed to the test results) shouldn't be anything to worry about. However, if, when adequately prepared, the test-taker still panics, blanks out, or seems to overreact, this is not a fully rational reaction. While this can be considered normal too, there are many ways to combat and overcome these effects.

Remember that anxiety cannot be entirely eliminated, however, there are ways to minimize it, to make the anxiety easier to manage. Preparation is one of the best ways to minimize test anxiety. Therefore the following techniques are wise in order to best fight off any anxiety that may want to build.

To begin with, try to avoid cramming before a test, whenever it is possible. By trying to memorize an entire term's worth of information in one day, you'll be shocking your system, and not giving yourself a very good chance to absorb the information. This is an easy path to anxiety, so for those who suffer from test anxiety, cramming should not even be considered an option.

Instead of cramming, work throughout the semester to combine all of the material which is presented throughout the semester, and work on it gradually as the course goes by, making sure to master the main concepts first, leaving minor details for a week or so before the test.

To study for the upcoming exam, be sure to pose questions that may be on the examination, to gauge the ability to answer them by integrating the ideas from your texts, notes and lectures, as well as any supplementary readings.

If it is truly impossible to cover all of the information that was covered in that particular term, concentrate on the most important portions, that can be covered very well. Learn these concepts as best as possible, so that when the test comes, a goal can be made to use these concepts as presentations of your knowledge.

In addition to study habits, changes in attitude are critical to beating a struggle with test anxiety. In fact, an improvement of the perspective over the entire test-taking experience can actually help a test taker to enjoy studying and therefore improve the overall experience. Be certain not to overemphasize the significance of the grade - know that the result of the test is neither a reflection of self worth, nor is it a measure of intelligence; one grade will not predict a person's future success.

To improve an overall testing outlook, the following steps should be tried:
- Keeping in mind that the most reasonable expectation for taking a test is to expect to try to demonstrate as much of what you know as you possibly can.
- Reminding ourselves that a test is only one test; this is not the only one, and there will be others.
- The thought of thinking of oneself in an irrational, all-or-nothing term should be avoided at all costs.
- A reward should be designated for after the test, so there's something to look forward to. Whether it be going to a movie, going out to eat, or simply visiting friends, schedule it in advance, and do it no matter what result is expected on the exam.

Test-takers should also keep in mind that the basics are some of the most important things, even beyond anti-anxiety techniques and studying. Never neglect the basic social, emotional and biological needs, in order to try to absorb information. In order to best achieve, these three factors must be held as just as important as the studying itself.

Study Steps

Remember the following important steps for studying:

- Maintain healthy nutrition and exercise habits. Continue both your recreational activities and social pass times. These both contribute to your physical and emotional well being.

- Be certain to get a good amount of sleep, especially the night before the test, because when you're overtired you are not able to perform to the best of your best ability.

- Keep the studying pace to a moderate level by taking breaks when they are needed, and varying the work whenever possible, to keep the mind fresh instead of getting bored.

- When enough studying has been done that all the material that can be learned has been learned, and the test taker is prepared for the test, stop studying and do something relaxing such as listening to music, watching a movie, or taking a warm bubble bath.

There are also many other techniques to minimize the uneasiness or apprehension that is experienced along with test anxiety before, during, or even after the examination. In fact, there are a great deal of things that can be done to stop anxiety from interfering with lifestyle and performance. Again, remember that anxiety will not be eliminated entirely, and it shouldn't be. Otherwise that "up" feeling for exams would not exist, and most of us depend on that sensation to perform better than usual. However, this anxiety has to be at a level that is manageable.

Of course, as we have just discussed, being prepared for the exam is half the battle right away. Attending all classes, finding out what knowledge will be expected on the exam, and knowing the exam schedules are easy steps to lowering anxiety. Keeping up with work will remove the need to cram, and efficient study habits will eliminate wasted time. Studying should be done in an ideal location for concentration, so that it is simple to become interested in the material and give it complete attention. A method such as SQ3R (Survey, Question, Read, Recite, Review) is a wonderful key to follow to make sure that the study habits are as effective as possible, especially in the case of learning from a textbook. Flashcards are great techniques for memorization. Learning to take good notes will mean that notes will be full of useful information, so that less sifting will need to be done to seek out what is pertinent for studying. Reviewing notes after class and then again on occasion will keep the information fresh in the mind. From notes that have been taken summary sheets and outlines can be made for simpler reviewing.

A study group can also be a very motivational and helpful place to study, as there will be a sharing of ideas, all of the minds can work together, to make sure that everyone understands, and the studying will be made more interesting because it will be a social occasion.

Basically, though, as long as the test-taker remains organized and self confident, with efficient study habits, less time will need to be spent studying, and higher grades will be achieved.

To become self confident, there are many useful steps. The first of these is "self talk." It has been shown through extensive research, that self-talk for students who suffer from test anxiety, should be well monitored, in order to make sure that it contributes to self confidence as opposed to sinking the student. Frequently the self talk of test-anxious students is negative or self-defeating, thinking that everyone else is smarter and faster, that they always mess up, and that if they don't do well, they'll fail the entire course. It is important to decreasing anxiety that awareness is made of self talk. Try writing any negative self thoughts and then disputing them with a positive statement instead. Begin self-encouragement as though it was a friend speaking. Repeat positive statements to help reprogram the mind to believing in successes instead of failures.

Helpful Techniques

Other extremely helpful techniques include:

- Self-visualization of doing well and reaching goals
- While aiming for an "A" level of understanding, don't try to "overprotect" by setting your expectations lower. This will only convince the mind to stop studying in order to meet the lower expectations.
- Don't make comparisons with the results or habits of other students. These are individual factors, and different things work for different people, causing different results.
- Strive to become an expert in learning what works well, and what can be done in order to improve. Consider collecting this data in a journal.
- Create rewards for after studying instead of doing things before studying that will only turn into avoidance behaviors.
- Make a practice of relaxing - by using methods such as progressive relaxation, self-hypnosis, guided imagery, etc - in order to make relaxation an automatic sensation.
- Work on creating a state of relaxed concentration so that concentrating will take on the focus of the mind, so that none will be wasted on worrying.
- Take good care of the physical self by eating well and getting enough sleep.
- Plan in time for exercise and stick to this plan.

Beyond these techniques, there are other methods to be used before, during and after the test that will help the test-taker perform well in addition to overcoming anxiety.

Before the exam comes the academic preparation. This involves establishing a study schedule and beginning at least one week before the actual date of the test. By doing this, the anxiety of not having enough time to study for the test will be automatically eliminated. Moreover, this will make the studying a much more effective experience, ensuring that the learning will be an easier process. This relieves much undue pressure on the test-taker.

Summary sheets, note cards, and flash cards with the main concepts and examples of these main concepts should be prepared in advance of the actual studying time. A topic should never be eliminated from this process. By omitting a topic because it isn't expected to be on the test is only setting up the test-taker for anxiety should it actually appear on the exam. Utilize the course syllabus for laying out the topics that should be studied. Carefully go over the notes that were made in class, paying special attention to any of the issues that the professor took special care to emphasize while lecturing in class. In the textbooks, use the chapter review, or if possible, the chapter tests, to begin your review.

It may even be possible to ask the instructor what information will be covered on the exam, or what the format of the exam will be (for example, multiple choice, essay, free form, true-false). Additionally, see if it is possible to find out how many questions will be on the test. If a review sheet or sample test has been offered by the professor, make good use of it, above anything else, for the preparation for the test. Another great resource for getting to know the examination is reviewing tests from previous semesters. Use these tests to review, and aim to achieve a 100% score on each of the possible topics. With a few exceptions, the goal that you set for yourself is the highest one that you will reach.

Take all of the questions that were assigned as homework, and rework them to any other possible course material. The more problems reworked, the more skill and confidence will form as a result. When forming the solution to a problem, write out each of the steps. Don't simply do head work. By doing as many steps on paper as possible, much clarification and therefore confidence will be formed. Do this with as many homework problems as possible, before checking the answers. By checking the answer after each problem, a reinforcement will exist, that will not be on the exam. Study situations should be as exam-like as possible, to prime the test-taker's system for the experience. By waiting to check the answers at the end, a psychological advantage will be formed, to decrease the stress factor.

Another fantastic reason for not cramming is the avoidance of confusion in concepts, especially when it comes to mathematics. 8-10 hours of study will become one hundred percent more effective if it is spread out over a week or at least several days, instead of doing it all in one sitting. Recognize that the human brain requires time in order to assimilate new material, so frequent breaks and a span of study time over several days will be much more beneficial.

Additionally, don't study right up until the point of the exam. Studying should stop a minimum of one hour before the exam begins. This allows the brain to rest and put things in their proper order. This will also provide the time to become as relaxed as possible when going into the examination room. The test-taker will also have time to eat well and eat sensibly. Know that the brain needs food as much as the rest of the body. With enough food and enough sleep, as well as a relaxed attitude, the body and the mind are primed for success.

Avoid any anxious classmates who are talking about the exam. These students only spread anxiety, and are not worth sharing the anxious sentimentalities.

Before the test also involves creating a positive attitude, so mental preparation should also be a point of concentration. There are many keys to creating a positive attitude. Should fears become rushing in, make a visualization of taking the exam, doing well, and seeing an A written on the paper. Write out a list of affirmations that will bring a feeling of confidence, such as "I am doing well in my English class," "I studied well and know my material," "I enjoy this class." Even if the affirmations aren't believed at first, it sends a positive message to the subconscious which will result in an alteration of the overall belief system, which is the system that creates reality.

If a sensation of panic begins, work with the fear and imagine the very worst! Work through the entire scenario of not passing the test, failing the entire course, and dropping out of school, followed by not getting a job, and pushing a shopping cart through the dark alley where you'll live. This will place things into perspective! Then, practice deep breathing and create a visualization of the opposite situation - achieving an "A" on the exam, passing the entire course, receiving the degree at a graduation ceremony.

On the day of the test, there are many things to be done to ensure the best results, as well as the most calm outlook. The following stages are suggested in order to maximize test-taking potential:

- Begin the examination day with a moderate breakfast, and avoid any coffee or beverages with caffeine if the test taker is prone to jitters. Even people who are used to managing caffeine can feel jittery or light-headed when it is taken on a test day.

- Attempt to do something that is relaxing before the examination begins. As last minute cramming clouds the mastering of overall concepts, it is better to use this time to create a calming outlook.

- Be certain to arrive at the test location well in advance, in order to provide time to select a location that is away from doors, windows and other distractions, as well as giving enough time to relax before the test begins.

- Keep away from anxiety generating classmates who will upset the sensation of stability and relaxation that is being attempted before the exam.

- Should the waiting period before the exam begins cause anxiety, create a self-distraction by reading a light magazine or something else that is relaxing and simple.

During the exam itself, read the entire exam from beginning to end, and find out how much time should be allotted to each individual problem. Once writing the exam, should more time be taken for a problem, it should be abandoned, in order to begin another problem. If there is time at the end, the unfinished problem can always be returned to and completed.

Read the instructions very carefully - twice - so that unpleasant surprises won't follow during or after the exam has ended.

When writing the exam, pretend that the situation is actually simply the completion of homework within a library, or at home. This will assist in forming a relaxed atmosphere, and will allow the brain extra focus for the complex thinking function.

Begin the exam with all of the questions with which the most confidence is felt. This will build the confidence level regarding the entire exam and will begin a quality momentum. This will also create encouragement for trying the problems where uncertainty resides.

Going with the "gut instinct" is always the way to go when solving a problem. Second guessing should be avoided at all costs. Have confidence in the ability to do well.

For essay questions, create an outline in advance that will keep the mind organized and make certain that all of the points are remembered. For multiple choice, read every answer, even if the correct one has been spotted - a better one may exist.

Continue at a pace that is reasonable and not rushed, in order to be able to work carefully. Provide enough time to go over the answers at the end, to check for small errors that can be corrected.

Should a feeling of panic begin, breathe deeply, and think of the feeling of the body releasing sand through its pores. Visualize a calm, peaceful place, and include all of the sights, sounds and sensations of this image. Continue the deep breathing, and take a few minutes to continue this with closed eyes. When all is well again, return to the test.

If a "blanking" occurs for a certain question, skip it and move on to the next question. There will be time to return to the other question later. Get everything done that can be done, first, to guarantee all the grades that can be compiled, and to build all of the confidence possible. Then return to the weaker questions to build the marks from there.

Remember, one's own reality can be created, so as long as the belief is there, success will follow. And remember: anxiety can happen later, right now, there's an exam to be written!

After the examination is complete, whether there is a feeling for a good grade or a bad grade, don't dwell on the exam, and be certain to follow through on the reward that was promised...and enjoy it! Don't dwell on any mistakes that have been made, as there is nothing that can be done at this point anyway.

Additionally, don't begin to study for the next test right away. Do something relaxing for a while, and let the mind relax and prepare itself to begin absorbing information again.

From the results of the exam - both the grade and the entire experience, be certain to learn from what has gone on. Perfect studying habits and work some more on confidence in order to make the next examination experience even better than the last one.

Learn to avoid places where openings occurred for laziness, procrastination and day dreaming.

Use the time between this exam and the next one to better learn to relax, even learning to relax on cue, so that any anxiety can be controlled during the next exam. Learn how to relax the body. Slouch in your chair if that helps. Tighten and then relax all of the different muscle groups, one group at a time, beginning with the feet and then working all the way up to the neck and face. This will ultimately relax the muscles more than they were to begin with. Learn how to breathe deeply and comfortably, and focus on this breathing going in and out as a relaxing thought. With every exhale, repeat the word "relax."

As common as test anxiety is, it is very possible to overcome it. Make yourself one of the test-takers who overcome this frustrating hindrance.

Special Report: Retaking the Test: What Are Your Chances at Improving Your Score?

After going through the experience of taking a major test, many test takers feel that once is enough. The test usually comes during a period of transition in the test taker's life, and taking the test is only one of a series of important events. With so many distractions and conflicting recommendations, it may be difficult for a test taker to rationally determine whether or not he should retake the test after viewing his scores.

The importance of the test usually only adds to the burden of the retake decision. However, don't be swayed by emotion. There a few simple questions that you can ask yourself to guide you as you try to determine whether a retake would improve your score:

1. What went wrong? Why wasn't your score what you expected?

Can you point to a single factor or problem that you feel caused the low score? Were you sick on test day? Was there an emotional upheaval in your life that caused a distraction? Were you late for the test or not able to use the full time allotment? If you can point to any of these specific, individual problems, then a retake should definitely be considered.

2. Is there enough time to improve?

Many problems that may show up in your score report may take a lot of time for improvement. A deficiency in a particular math skill may require weeks or months of tutoring and studying to improve. If you have enough time to improve an identified weakness, then a retake should definitely be considered.

3. How will additional scores be used? Will a score average, highest score, or most recent score be used?

Different test scores may be handled completely differently. If you've taken the test multiple times, sometimes your highest score is used, sometimes your average score is computed and used, and sometimes your most recent score is used. Make sure you understand what method will be used to evaluate your scores, and use that to help you determine whether a retake should be considered.

4. Are my practice test scores significantly higher than my actual test score?

If you have taken a lot of practice tests and are consistently scoring at a much higher level than your actual test score, then you should consider a retake. However, if you've taken five practice tests and only one of your scores was higher than your actual test score, or if your practice test scores were only slightly higher than your actual test score, then it is unlikely that you will significantly increase your score.

5. Do I need perfect scores or will I be able to live with this score? Will this score still allow me to follow my dreams?

What kind of score is acceptable to you? Is your current score "good enough?" Do you have to have a certain score in order to pursue the future of your dreams? If you won't be happy with your current score, and there's no way that you could live with it, then you should consider a retake. However, don't get your hopes up. If you are looking for significant improvement, that may or may not be possible. But if you won't be happy otherwise, it is at least worth the effort.

Remember that there are other considerations. To achieve your dream, it is likely that your grades may also be taken into account. A great test score is usually not the only thing necessary to succeed. Make sure that you aren't overemphasizing the importance of a high test score.

Furthermore, a retake does not always result in a higher score. Some test takers will score lower on a retake, rather than higher. One study shows that one-fourth of test takers will achieve a significant improvement in test score, while one-sixth of test takers will actually show a decrease. While this shows that most test takers will improve, the majority will only improve their scores a little and a retake may not be worth the test taker's effort.

Finally, if a test is taken only once and is considered in the added context of good grades on the part of a test taker, the person reviewing the grades and scores may be tempted to assume that the test taker just had a bad day while taking the test, and may discount the low test score in favor of the high grades. But if the test is retaken and the scores are approximately the same, then the validity of the low scores are only confirmed. Therefore, a retake could actually hurt a test taker by definitely bracketing a test taker's score ability to a limited range.